The Conscript Army

Inequality in Society

General Editor: Frank Field

The Conscript Army
A Study of Britain's Unemployed

Edited by
Frank Field

Routledge & Kegan Paul
London, Henley and Boston

First published in 1977
by Routledge & Kegan Paul Ltd
39 Store Street,
London WC1E 7DD,
Broadway House,
Newtown Road,
Henley-on-Thames,
Oxon RG9 1EN and
9 Park Street,
Boston, Mass. 02108, USA
Set in 9/11 pt Baskerville by
Computacomp (UK) Ltd, Fort William, Scotland
and printed in Great Britain by
Lowe & Brydone Printers Ltd.
Thetford, Norfolk

British Library Cataloguing in Publication Data

The conscript army. – (Inequality in society).

1. Unemployed – Great Britain
I. Field, Frank, b.1942 II. Series
331.1'37941   HD5767.A6   77–30325

ISBN 0 7100 8779 9

Contents

To Adrian Sinfield

Contributors

Louie Burghes studied Sociology at London University. She worked for over two years in the Urban Deprivation Unit of the Home Office as a Research Officer before joining Frank Field as his Personal Assistant.

Frank Field taught in the London Colleges of Further Education in Southwark and Hammersmith before joining the Child Poverty Action Group in 1969. In 1966 he contested the Buckinghamshire South constituency seat for the Labour Party and was a councillor in Hounslow for four years. He has edited *Twentieth Century State Education*, *Black Britons*, *Low Pay*, *Education and the Urban Crisis* and *Are Low Wages Inevitable?* He is the author of *Unequal Britian* and co-author of *To Him Who Hath*. Since 1974 he has also been Director of the Low Pay Unit.

Clare Dennehy is the Secretary of the Child Poverty Action Group.

Steve Hannah is a lecturer in economics at Keele University.

Chris Pond studied Economics at the University of Sussex and worked in the Department of Economics at Birkbeck College, London, before taking up his present post as Research Officer at the Low Pay Unit. He has contributed to *Inflation and Low Incomes*, *Trade Unions and Taxation*, *Are Low Wages Inevitable?* and is co-author of *To Him Who Hath*.

Jill Sullivan is the Secretary of the Low Pay Unit. She is the author of *The Brush Off*, a study of low pay among cleaners.

Stephen Winyard studied Economics and Social Policy at Essex University. He worked as a Research Officer in the Social Services Department of Kingston-upon-Thames before joining the Low Pay Unit where he worked for two and a half years as a Research Officer. He is now lecturing in Social Administration at Preston Polytechnic. He has contributed to *Low Pay*, *Are Low Wages Inevitable?* and *Trade Unions and Taxation*.

Introduction

Frank Field

The public outcry against unemployment has been anaesthetised by a prolonged and sustained campaign to convince us that unemployment in the 1970s is, in important respects, fundamentally different from that in any other time. We are told that the unemployment figures do not really mean what they appear to tell us and, even if they did, that the link between unemployment and poverty has been irreparably broken. And, as if this wasn't enough, public attention is drawn to the supposed workshy and scroungers who, it is alleged, make up one in five of the unemployed, but who are rarely named.

It has been a truly remarkable campaign, particularly when one stands back and thinks how important work is and always has been to the vast majority of human beings. An American writer expressed its importance in the following terms: 'So closely is work tied in with the social and psychological development of man that it is almost impossible to think what it means to be human without thinking of work' (Elliot Liebow, 1970). The current campaign has been successful both in smothering the anger of the unemployed at the way in which we deny them a useful and dignified role in the community, and driving a wedge between the unemployed and the rest of society. From across this chasm the unemployed hear accusations not only of their being workshy, but also at their having a standard of living in excess of many members of the working community.

Few human beings can live with themselves for any length of time knowing the dreadful truth that they are unwanted by the society of which they are members. People living with a public declaration about their lack of use adopt a network of protective practices. Some withdraw, isolating themselves from their families and the rest of the community. When we were carrying out our survey in Liverpool, which is reported in chapter 5, we were struck by the way that the unemployed man's wife was often prepared to talk while her husband hovered silently in the background. Wives told us of their husbands' fear of being pointed out in the street as unemployed. Trips out of the house were so curtailed that some wives had difficulty in persuading their husbands to continue signing on at the employment exchange.

Other unemployed people throw up a totally different protective shield. They manage to live with the self-recrimination which so often accompanies unemployment by making out that being workless is something they positively welcome. This self-spun chain-mail is difficult to pierce during an interview, and yet when work is offered these people are seen to be scrambling, along with everyone else, for those few jobs which are available. One well-known claimants' leader, who used to bring the house down with applause when he declared that work was redundant, eagerly seized the first job which was offered to him. When asked on what he was going to spend his pay packet, the claimant replied that he was saving up to buy new sets of clothes. Fearing renewed unemployment he wanted adequate stocks so that he would never be forced into 'begging' for clothing grants from the Supplementary Benefits Commission.

A different response comes from some others of the unemployed who react similarly to some sections of the working population. Denis Marsden describes the reaction of such men living in areas where there are large numbers of unemployed and few job opportunities. In these circumstances the local employment exchanges, having only a handful of jobs on their books, are unable to send unemployed workers regularly for interviews. Marsden reports on some claimants who demand that the authorities should take tougher action against themselves – as though this will somehow produce more jobs. (Denis Marsden and Euan Duff, 1975, p.249) Only a full understanding of the misery and deprivation of unemployment can explain these self-destructive reactions. One objective of this book is to re-emphasise the individual suffering of the unemployed who all too often are known only as cold, numbing statistics.

The other aims of this book are ambitious – to challenge the mythology perpetuated by those who would have us believe that unemployment is a reflection of individual shortcomings rather than a direct result of government policy, to re-arm the unemployed with the facts to combat the ever-present stigma in their lives and to re-assert the belief that, in a civilised society, nothing less than full employment is acceptable. In the debate about unemployment one voice has been conspicuous by its absence. We hope that this book may play its part in helping the unemployed to concentrate less on building protective shields against a hostile world and concentrate their energies more in helping to change those policies from which their misfortune stems.

A number of people have helped in producing this book. Clare Dennehy has been largely responsible for preparing the manuscript for publication although she has been helped in this by Jill Sullivan. David

Jordan kindly read through to check the typescript and in doing so suggested numerous changes which strengthen the presentation of the argument, particularly in the chapters which I wrote. Michael Meacher MP also read and commented upon part of the manuscript. Members of the Low Pay Unit, together with Lesley Day, Clare Dennehy and Chris Trinder, undertook the fieldwork for the small survey in Liverpool and were helped in this by Marie Brown.

We are grateful to members of the Eleanor Rathbone Society who helped to arrange the interviewing in Liverpool. We should also like to record the help given to us by a number of MPs: Lynda Chalker, Bruce George, Neil Kinnock, Jo Richardson, Richard Wainwright and particularly Peter Bottomley, although none of these Members will necessarily subscribe to the interpretation we have placed on the material they obtained from Parliamentary Questions. To this list we should like to add one other person. This book is dedicated to Adrian Sinfield from whom all the contributors have learned so much about the unemployment question.

We are tearing our guts out with incredible accusations that a group of people living on legally approved benefits are threatening to destroy our whole society. The state is in danger because some people who are being paid unemployment benefit don't try to get a job, which isn't there anyway. This is despite the government having deliberately devised an economic programme to create unemployment. Unemployed people are less dangerous to the economy than those earning and spending money. The fewer than two in 100 who can get more on benefit than in the underpaid, underskilled jobs which are all they could get, if they were there in the first place, are a small price to pay. The rest ought to get a service medal for being on the dole. They are the conscripts in the war against inflation.

Catherine Carmichael
New Society, 20 January 1977

1 Making sense of the unemployment figures

Frank Field

Over recent years there has been a growing debate as to whether the figures published by the Department of Employment overestimate the numbers of unemployed. Broadly speaking there are three reasons why the unemployment figures are criticised as being an unreliable guide to the numbers of persons wishing to obtain work. First, there have been those arguments presented by what has become known as the monetarist school. This group holds that it is no longer possible to obtain full employment (as most people understand the term) by applying Keynesian remedies. It is claimed that there has been a major change in the structure of the labour market breaking the link between an increase in aggregate demand and the automatic increase in the number of jobs. In Chapter 3 we look at this argument in detail and try to estimate the numbers of persons who are made unemployed by inadequate total aggregate demand compared to other forces which may be at work.

Second, and often allied with the first group, have been those who argue that it is necessary to have a higher level of unemployment if we are to bring inflation under control. Linked with this argument has been the contention that an increase in unemployment does not now mean an increase in the number of poor and deprived. Two views are put forward in support if this standpoint. First, it is argued that the introduction of earnings-related unemployment benefit and redundancy payments have increased the numbers voluntarily unemployed – and have swollen the nominal size of the register. A higher level of increased unemployment is therefore needed to have the same impact on wage rates. Second, the proponents of this school of thought suggest that recent welfare reforms have taken the financial sting out of unemployment – hence government should not worry about using high unemployment to run the economy. We will be examining the validity of this argument in Chapter 3.

There has also been a third force at work in the current debate. A number of critics who believe that the link between unemployment and poverty has been broken by generous welfare reforms, as well as arguing that there has been a fundamental change in the relationship between unemployment and vacancies, have gone on to allege that the official unemployment figures grossly overestimate the numbers of unemployed. Explaining away the unemployed has been tried before; Sir Horace Wilson, the Permanent Secretary at the Ministry of Labour until 1930, spent much of his time during the interwar years showing that there was almost no unemployment worth talking about once one had revised the official figures. A similar campaign is being orchestrated today. It is argued that five groups of unemployed claimants should be removed from the unemployment figures, as they cannot be described as 'genuinely unemployed'.

The main part of this chapter is concerned with analysing the arguments put forward for deducting these five groups from the unemployment figures. We conclude by suggesting that far from overestimating the numbers of unemployed, the data issued by the Department of Employment each month significantly underestimate the numbers of persons who wish to work.

Each month the Department of Employment (DE) publishes data on the numbers registered at their local offices as unemployed. The count, as it is called, includes everyone who has reported to a local employment exchange that he or she is seeking work and has been classified by local officers as being 'capable and available for work'. It therefore includes those who are entitled to unemployment benefit and/or supplementary benefit as well as those not claiming benefit but who are 'seeking work and capable of obtaining work'.

Recently two changes have been made to the data. Following a report by an interdepartmental working party, the numbers of the 'temporary stop' are shown separately. The temporary stopped category covers those workers who have been suspended by their employer on the understanding that they will shortly resume work. (*Unemployment Statistics,* 1972) More recently the numbers of students registering for benefit during the vacations have also been excluded from the wholly unemployed. However, critics maintain that on five counts these data still overestimate the numbers of people who are unemployed. We look at each of these criticisms in turn.

School leavers

John Wood was one of the first people to question how accurate a gauge are the official unemployment figures of the numbers of persons seeking work. (Wood, 1972) He drew attention to the fact that the unemployment register includes, not unexpectedly, school leavers who have not yet found employment. Every year about half a million young people enter the labour market for the first time and, over recent years, an increasing number of them have found it difficult to find employment. At the time of writing Wood pointed out that in the three months from July between 35,000 and 55,000 school leavers are included as unemployed although, by the end of the year, the figure is generally down to 3,000 to 4,000.

In calculating the size of the labour force, Wood and others add in the numbers of school leavers who have successfully found work. They therefore increase the base upon which the percentage on unemployed is calculated, but they go on to exclude unemployed school leavers from their total of the unemployed. This adjustment to the unemployment figures cannot be justified by what is happening in the labour market. As school leavers are not eligible for unemployment pay (although they could be drawing supplementary benefit) one of their main reasons for registering is to obtain work, and this group is as much part of the labour force, albeit unemployed for part of the time, as any other group of workers. As we see in the following chapter unemployment is affecting this group of the labour force to an increasing extent. Highlighting this trend, A.J.H. Dean observes that

> the fact that over 5 per cent of those who left school in search of employment at the end of the 1974/5 school year were still unemployed nine months later indicates that the problem of the unemployed school leavers is now one of a more serious order of magnitude than just the previous temporary peaking phenomenon. (Dean, 1976, p. 63)

Unsuitable for regular full-time work

Both Sam Brittan and the Centre for Policy Studies maintain that, as a considerable number of the unemployed are unsuitable for full-time work, their numbers should be excluded from the unemployment statistics. How valid is this charge? Sam Brittan has written,

> Another element that swells the unemployment figures is the inclusion of approximately 30 per cent of the unemployed who have been classified as both 'poor prospects and unenthusiastic', meaning not that they are strictly unemployable but they take longer to obtain jobs and find it more difficult to hold on to them'. (Brittan, 1975, p. 70)

He then goes on to state: 'The purpose of trying to estimate their numbers is not to minimise their plight or question their right to benefit, but to emphasise that they provide a misleading guide to the state of the labour market and therefore to monetary and fiscal policy.' (*ibid.*, p.70)

The Centre for Policy Studies makes a similar point. It calls attention to those who are registered as unemployed but unable to hold down regular, full-time work. And it concludes:

> On the basis of surveys carried out by the Department of Employment

in 1973 and 1974 it is calculated that approximately 30 per cent of the registered unemployed fall into this category, or into the 'somewhat unenthusiastic' category, or both. Since it is unrealistic to suppose that this proportion remains constant with the official figures above the one million and a quarter mark, the figure arrived at by this method has been adjusted downwards and it has been further revised to avoid including any of the occupational pensioners (which are also deducted from the total). (Centre for Policy Studies, 1976)

But does information from the DE support this view on the numbers unable to hold down full-time employment even if it was offered to them?

In the first place the surveys by the Department make plain that they exclude those from the survey who obtain special or temporary registration. These are the people who 'were expected to get jobs very quickly'. It is therefore wrong to allege that 30 per cent of all unemployed are unlikely to hold down full-time jobs should they be offered. In addition a careful reading of the survey material presents a very different picture. True, the Department believes that 'in the assessment of local office staff one third of unemployed men (in the survey) are "somewhat unenthusiastic" for work.' (DE, 1974a, 212) However, the Department stresses that it is 'particularly important not to draw too strong an inference from answers to [this] question ... in isolation [for] this does not mean that those men would in practice refuse a job if one was offered them.' (*ibid.*, p.212) The DE goes on to note that not only would they be in danger of losing benefit if they refused a job offered to them but, more importantly, in a follow-up survey about a third of these men had found employment during the intervening six months.

It has also been pointed out that the number of so-called unemployable varies with the level of employment. Examining the data on the numbers of unemployed males who it was alleged had poor employment prospects for personal reasons in 1964 and 1973, James Hughes has noted 'that while the proportion of male unemployed remained remarkably stable the actual number involved almost doubled, from 143,000 to 262,000.' Hughes went on to conclude: 'This suggests that the number actually classified as having poor prospects of securing long term employment (i.e. the so-called unemployables) is dependent upon the overall level of unemployment which itself reflects the demand for labour.' (Hughes, 1975, p.327)

The interdepartmental working party on unemployment statistics made a similar point. They commented that there is 'some confusion between the meaning of "unemployable" as a description of certain characteristics of a person, and as a description of the "employability" of a person in a particular labour market.' (*Unemployment Statistics*, 1972, p.18) In other words, people become more or less employable depending on the demand for labour, although their personal characteristics remain unchanged. Those who call for deducting the unemployables from the unemployment figures are therefore shown to be involved in a circular argument. As unemployment rises, more and more marginal workers find themselves registering for work with the Department of Employment. Their alleged unemployability, which is itself a product of the level of demand for labour, is then used to argue for their exclusion from the official figures.

The short-term unemployed

The third group who critics argue should be excluded from the total of unemployed are those who are changing jobs, or the frictionally unemployed. The Centre for Policy Studies argues that,

> Even during periods of comparatively full employment significant numbers of people will be 'frictionally' or temporarily out of work. Since a growing economy requires change, including change in the distribution of labour, this is inevitably so. The figure for those 'just changing jobs' has been taken as those on the register for less than four weeks. (Centre for Policy Studies, 1976, pp.4–5)

Sam Brittan puts forward a similar argument. 'The main focus of social concern in the monthly count should be concentrated on those who do *not* succeed in getting a job within a few weeks.' (Brittan, 1975, p.69) However, he does note that the proportion of the unemployed out of work for four weeks or less has been falling, but it 'is still large enough to account for over 170,000 of the Great Britain total' in March 1975. (*ibid.*, pp.69–70) How accurate is the argument maintaining that those unemployed for four weeks or less are a guide to the numbers suffering short-term or transitional unemployment?

After analysing all the available data, the Working Party concluded that 'it is not possible to identify those on the register at a particular time who will obtain employment within a given time in the future'. (*Unemployment Statistics*, 1972, p.13) Hughes has also considered how accurate a guide to frictional unemployment are the short-term unemployed as defined by the DE count. He suggests that an analysis of unemployment in vacancies by occupation or skill is much more likely to give a realistic measure, as a frictionally unemployed worker is one that is, by definition, one for whom a vacancy exists. In this analysis Hughes defines short-term unemployment as those on the register for eight weeks or less. After a study of occupational unemployment and vacancy data he writes, 'that the number of frictionally unemployed is considerably less than the measure of short-term unemployment derived from the duration statistics'. And he adds,

> even if a case could be made for subtracting the frictionally
> unemployed from the unemployment count – and it is not accepted by
> the present writer that such a case can be made – to exclude all those
> who have been unemployed for up to eight weeks will lead to an
> underestimate of 'real' unemployment. (Hughes, 1975, p.324)

For example, in 1972 (the latest data presented in the analysis) he shows that there were 77,400 male frictionally unemployed compared with 192,200 who were defined as short-term unemployed.

There is an additional reason why equating the short-term unemployed, as measured by the monthly snapshot taken by the Department of Employment, will lead to an overestimation of those frictionally unemployed. The Department's monthly snapshot inevitably includes some who suffer recurrent spells of short-term unemployment but, because of the nature of the count, cannot be identified. A recent survey by the DE suggested that 28 per cent of those unemployed in the middle of 1973 had two or more spells of unemployment in the previous twelve months. Almost 10 per cent had experienced three or more spells of unemployment during the same period. (DE, 1974c, p.449)

The critics are wrong to equate the short-term unemployed, as defined by the DE's monthly count, with being frictionally unemployed. The Department's own studies show that at any time at least a quarter of those who are defined as short term will also find themselves still unemployed after eight weeks. (DE, 1973a, pp.111–16) Moreover, the analysis by Hughes has shown that the numbers of short-term unemployed, who can also be legitimately classified as frictionally unemployed, fall as the total numbers of unemployed rise. But it is at this point in the trade cycle, when unemployment is growing, that there is most activity from the critics to revise downwards the real level of unemployment by equating the short-term unemployed with the frictionally unemployed. But as we do not claim that the count is any more than a gauge, albeit the best we have, of the numbers wishing to work and as we cannot categorise which of the unemployed will be frictionally unemployed as opposed to those who will be unemployed for other reasons at any one time, there are no legitimate grounds for excluding this group.

The voluntarily unemployed

Critics maintain that two other groups of the unemployed should be discounted when considering the true level of unemployment. The first and most bizarre suggestion comes from Jim Boulet and Adrian Bell, who have proposed that those on the register for between eight and twenty-six weeks should be excluded, as they are voluntarily unemployed. (Boulet and Bell, 1973, p.12) No reasons are given either to support the accusation, or to justify the cut-off points of eight and twenty-six weeks. One can understand why they picked a lower limit of eight weeks. In common with other critics Boulet and Bell argue that those on the unemployment register for up to eight weeks should be excluded because they are frictionally unemployed, although we have earlier criticised such an approach. But no reason is put forward in their work for a cut-off point of twenty-six weeks. Although it is true that those who are fortunate enough to claim earnings-related benefits cease to draw this supplement after six months, there is no evidence anywhere to suggest that those who are unemployed up to six months choose to be so. As Hughes has dryly noted, 'Had they extended it [the cut-off point] to 104 weeks they could have reduced "real unemployment" to almost zero.' (Hughes, 1975, p.325)

Other critics have concentrated their fire on the numbers of occupational pensioners on the register, suggesting that the number of voluntarily unemployed occupational pensioners is unlikely to be less than 30,000. Boulet and Bell have put the total slightly lower at 25,000. (Boulet and Bell, 1973) Similarly the Centre for Policy Studies has written,

> It is currently estimated that of the 50–60,000 people between 60 and 65 who have retired on occupational pensions and who register as unemployed, approximately 30,000 do so primarily to obtain national insurance credits or social benefits and not to obtain work. In doing so they are only following official procedure, but there is no reason why they should be regarded as unemployed. (Centre for Policy Studies, 1976, p.5)

While accepting that a number of occupational pensioners may register as unemployed primarily to gain the national insurance credits, it is legitimate to ask why this group has been subtracted from the total of unemployed. Again careful reading of the survey data shows that 58 per cent of occupational pensioners have recently been made unemployed (they are therefore claiming unemployment benefit or are so poor that they are claiming supplementary benefit). Furthermore, a quarter were drawing an occupational pension valued at less than £5 a week. The financial circumstances of a large proportion of this group are such that if employment opportunities were offered, many claimants would seize them. (DE, 1974a, p.214)

Again the critics' case is not proven and they are involved in a self-fulfilling prophecy. As unemployment rises, those groups most at risk, such as the elderly, have less chance of obtaining work. Because they have little chance of obtaining work the critics argue that they should be excluded from the numbers of unemployed. But most people would consider that not being able to obtain work is what unemployment is all about.

Fraudulent claims

The fifth group who it is claimed should be excluded from the total of registered unemployed are those who it is alleged are claiming benefit fraudulently. Boulet and Bell's estimate puts the numbers fraudulently claiming benefit at 130,000 for January 1972 (p.14), while Sir Keith Joseph has alleged that probably 'one in ten of those registered unemployed fraudulently draw benefit at normal times.' (Joseph, 1974) John Wood suggests that 100,000 were 'falsely unemployed' and Sam Brittan concluded that this total is 'likely to be right'. (Wood, 1972, p.59; and Brittan, 1975, p.73) How justified is this accusation?

In the first place it totally disregards the battery of control procedures the DHSS and DE have instituted in order to control the abuse of unemployment and social security payments. In Chapter 4 we detail all these checks against abuse, but it is important when considering the critics' estimates of the fraudulently unemployed to have some idea of their scope. The main control procedures are as follows:

1 A claimant may be suspended from benefit for leaving his last job or refusing a job without just cause. Nearly 400,000 claimants lost benefit for up to six weeks in 1975.
2 He may be interviewed by unemployment review officers. In 1975 164,533 interviews took place during which claimants had to account for their attempts to find work.
3 He may be sent for a medical examination. In 1974 5,483 medicals were carried out on claimants alleging they were too ill to work.
4 He may be required to attend a re-establishment centre, or sued for non-maintenance. Claimants may be paid benefit on condition they attend regularly at a re-establishment centre. Others are sued for not maintaining themselves and/or their family.
5 He can be checked by an unemployment review officer for the DE and a general investigator for the DHSS if it is alleged that a fraudulent claim is being made.

With this network of control procedures it is not surprising that official enquiries have shown that abuse of benefit by the unemployed is not taking place on the sort of scale the media suggest. When he was Secretary of State for Social Services, Sir Keith Joseph appointed Sir Henry Fisher to chair a committee to enquire into the abuse of social security benefits. The committee was told by the DE that in 1971–2 £101,960 was wrongly paid out in unemployment benefit. However, this total included overpayments by staff and, when one considers that a man with a wife and two children would then have been entitled to draw £727.50 a year flat-rate unemployment benefit, the numbers thought to be abusing benefit are put into perspective. (Fisher, 1973, p.51)

While abuse of benefit is wrong, its extent is not nearly as wide as many people believe. For example, a special enquiry carried out by the DE in local offices concentrated on those occupations where scope for drawing benefit and working on the side was greatest. In all 14,000 were covered by this special drive and 400 cases were established. Put another way, this enquiry showed that a little below 3 per cent of unemployed workers in receipt of unemployment benefit who were investigated were found to be making fraudulent claims. However, the Department makes clear that the sample was not a random one. They especially concentrated on those regions and those trades where they thought abuse to be most likely. Using these data, one observer has commented that if we assume about 70 per cent of the unemployed were drawing benefit, the maximum number of fraudulent claims would be about 19,000 in 1972. (Hughes, 1975, p.329) While this total is disturbing, it is, for the reasons outlined above, still likely to be an overestimate of the extent of fraud and is nowhere near the 100,000 to 130,000 fraudulent claims to benefit alleged to have occurred by some critics.

Again the argument that the numbers of unemployed grossly overestimate those available for work is not supported by the evidence. By its very nature, it is difficult to estimate the numbers who are unemployed and fraudulently claiming benefit. However, what evidence there is from government sources, a committee of enquiry, and independent research is ignored in favour of playing a 'hunch'. As with all the other groups which it is maintained should be deducted from the unemployment figures, we will only know the true extent of those who are unwilling to work when we have jobs which can be offered. That is the key test.

Estimating the true level of unemployment

By making dubious deductions from the numbers registered as unemployed each of the critics is able to reduce substantially the total numbers who, it is alleged, are 'really' unemployed. At a time when registered unemployment stood at 929,000, Wood managed to reduce this total to 346,000. The unemployment figure for March 1972 of 1,015,000 has been reduced to 532,000 'long-term unemployed' by Sam Brittan. An estimate given by the Centre for Policy Studies relating to July 1976 gives an unemployment level of 816,000 when the Department of Employment returns put the numbers at 1,463,000. As we have tried to show, none of the deductions by the critics can be supported by a careful evaluation of the available evidence. However misleading these revised totals of the numbers unemployed are, none of these critics reached the bizarre conclusion of Boulet and Bell who, in January 1972, estimated an unemployment level of *minus* 141,000 persons. Moreover, there is evidence that the figures published by the DE on the numbers of unemployed, far from exaggerating the numbers, underestimate considerably those who are unemployed and wishing to work. Some writers have focussed attention on the projections made by the DE about the growth of the labour market, and suggested that the failure of these projections to materialise is but one sign of 'hidden' unemployment. Others have drawn attention to data in the census and General Household Survey (GHS) to highlight a sizeable reserve army of unemployed who, because they are not entitled to benefit and/or have little hope of gaining a job through official channels, do not register themselves at the employment exchange.

The existence of this information is known to the critics. For example, the Centre for Policy Studies does not adjust the DE's figures to take account of them because 'it is impossible to say how many of them can be regarded as capable and available for work'. But the GHS only classifies individuals as unemployed if they describe themselves as seeking work. Why should a group which so describes itself, and about which we have more information from the GHS and the census than most of the groups which the critics deduct from the official data, be excluded when we try to gauge the numbers of unemployed? By examining the data we can see that this group amounts to a significant number of today's unemployed.

The census for 1966 shows that there were 103,500 men and 133,000 women who were economically active, but out of work and not registered as unemployed. In addition there were 120,000 men and 78,000 women also economically active, out of work and unregistered and who were unable to seek work at the time because of sickness.

The GHS also gives information on the numbers of unregistered unemployed. Of those describing themselves as seeking work in 1971, 7·5 per cent of men and 54 per cent of women had not registered as unemployed. Overall the survey found that the registered unemployed accounted for only 77·2 per cent of all unemployed persons. The GHS of 1972 found that 13·9 per cent of unemployed men and 53·2 per cent of unemployed females were not so registered at the employment exchange; in all 26·2 per cent of the unemployed had failed to register. A year later the GHS returned to this same question and showed that 20 per cent of males and 62 per cent of females who described themselves as unemployed were not registered at the employment exchange. Commenting on these figures, the GHS 'suggests a possible inverse relationship between the proportion of the unemployed who are unregistered and the total level of unemployment – i.e. as the overall rate of unemployment falls, the proportion who are unregistered rises'. (General Household Survey, 1976, p.63)

More recently the Department of Employment has produced estimates of the numbers of unregistered unemployed from the censuses and the General Household Surveys. Since the definitions of unemployed in the official count and the surveys are not the same, they have adjusted the former to provide comparable figures for the registered unemployed to those used in the surveys with their own definitions of unemployment.

The result has been to lower the official count for men and raise it for women. The figures obviously need to be treated with caution but they do give some idea of the numbers of people who are unemployed and yet fail to appear in the official count.

TABLE 1.1 *Numbers of unregistered unemployed*

	Summary of estimates of unregistered unemployment (000s)		
	Males	Females	Total
1966 Census of population (April)	90	120	170
1971 Census of population (April)	80	230	310
1971 GHS (annual average)	70	190	260
1972 GHS (annual average)	90	175	265
1973 GHS (annual average)	100	160	260

(*Source*: DE, 1976f, p. 1334)

The 1973 General Household Survey has published information on the steps which were being taken by unregistered unemployed persons to find work; 30 per cent of respondents placed advertisements or had replied to advertisements, 29 per cent had already made a direct approach to a prospective employer and 28 per cent were already awaiting the results of job applications. The evidence does show, therefore, that not only do the official unemployment figures seriously underestimate the numbers unemployed but that most of the non-registered workless are definitely seeking work.

Conclusion

In this first chapter we have attempted to separate a number of arguments which will be taken up and developed in this volume. Critics have tried to minimise the extent of unemployment either because they believe that social security provisions are so generous that there is no financial cost to the unemployed in running the economy at a higher level of unemployment, or they believe there is a link between high employment and rising prices. These key arguments are analysed in Chapters 3 and 7 respectively. Our purpose has been to examine carefully the reasons which have been put forward during the last few years, and always at a time of rising unemployment, to show that the total unemployment figures published by the Department of Employment each month do not give an accurate picture of those seeking work. We have attempted to show that these criticisms do not stand up to careful examination and that the only proper test which can be applied to most of those claimants who critics allege are not 'genuinely seeking work' is to offer them a job. Furthermore, there is a growing body of literature showing that the monthly returns from the Department of Employment, far from overestimating, actually underestimate significantly the numbers of persons actively seeking work. We have shown that in one year for which data exist the total of non-registered unemployed was as high as 310,000. Unemployment is one of the major economic and social ills we face as a community. Thus far we have concentrated on the overall unemployment figures. Next we turn our attention to those who compose Britain's growing army of unemployed.

2   Who are the unemployed?

Louie Burghes

Nearly one-and-a-half million people in Great Britian were unemployed in August 1976. Such a level of unemployment has not been experienced in this country since the 1930s. What do the unemployment figures tell us? Who are the unemployed? Are we all equally vulnerable to unemployment? Does it 'like ... God's gentle rain fall uniformly upon everyone ... '? (Liebow, 1970) This chapter will attempt to bring to life the unemployment figures by looking at the unemployed by sex, age, skill, region and race. But we will look first at the 'flows' of people onto and off the unemployment register and at the recurrence of unemployment and its duration.

The incidence of unemployment

In Chapter 1 the official unemployment data, the monthly 'counts', published by the Department of Employment were analysed. We concluded that not only are the accusations that the official figures overestimate the level of unemployment unfounded but also the count significantly underestimates the number of people who are unemployed. It is unfortunate, then, that in looking at who the unemployed are, we must throughout this chapter be almost wholly dependent on the official figures.

Over the last twenty years there has been a steady rise in the level of unemployment in Great Britain and we can see from Figure 2.1 that the rise has been dramatic in the last few years, reaching a million and a half in summer 1976. It is half-way to the unprecedented three million unemployed of 1933. The end of 1976 saw a slight fall in the total number of unemployed compared with the summer months; but it was only a temporary respite. The possibility of two million unemployed is no longer unrealistic. Figure 2.1 shows that while unemployment has continued to recover from its peaks as the economy picks up, the noticeable feature of the trend over the last twenty years has been the worsening of the peaks and the lessening of the improvement when it comes. Not only has the total number of unemployed been increasing

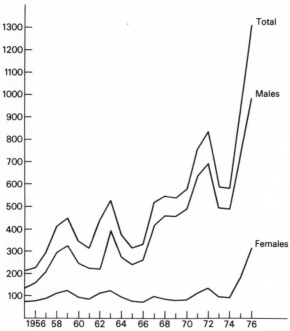

(*Sources*: DE, 1976a, tables 104 and 1977 table 105)

FIGURE 2.1 *Unemployment in Great Britain*

absolutely, but also as a proportion of the economically active population. In 1956 the unemployed were only 1·1 per cent of employees; by 1976 they had jumped to just over 4 per cent.

Flow statistics, recurring unemployment and its duration

The unemployment figures published monthly by the Department of Employment give a static 'snapshot' of the level of unemployment at a particular point in time. To some extent the picture is misleading. It is the flow statistics that tell us about the movement of people onto and off the register and they show the large monthly changes in the composition of the unemployed. And while in periods of rising or falling unemployment it is the difference between the inflow of people onto the register and the outflow of people off the register that account for the changes in the total numbers unemployed, the changes in the flows themselves are small in relation to the total change in the numbers unemployed.

Over the past ten years the monthly inflows and outflows have both been around 3–400,000. Even when unemployment is at very high levels the flows are generally within this range, with the changing level of unemployment caused by the small excesses of one flow over another. By the beginning of 1972, for example, registered unemployment was over 870,000; the excess of numbers joining the register over those leaving had at its maximum been about 25,000 in the spring of 1971. And as unemployment rose during 1975, there was an unprecedented excess of inflow over outflow, reaching about 50,000 in the summer, but still small in relation to the flows (320,000 to 380,000) and total unemployment.

While it is encouraging that outflows remain on as large a scale as they do even during periods of high unemployment, the flow statistics highlight two particularly important problems. First, the possibility that people may, and the evidence suggests do, suffer repeated spells of unemployment within short spaces of time. Second, that since in periods of high unemployment the excess of inflow over outflow is small in relation to the flows and to total unemployment, what we are witnessing at higher levels of unemployment is increasing duration of unemployment. We now turn and examine the evidence on both these issues. Their consequences for benefit entitlement are studied in the next chapter.

An analysis of the flow statistics suggested that as unemployment reaches high levels, some part of the increase is due to increasing duration of unemployment. However, the fact of a changing register, even when unemployment is high, suggests that some people may also be suffering recurring periods of unemployment.

There is, unfortunately, little evidence on the extent of repeated spells of unemployment. But two official surveys throw some light on the problem. In August 1961 the Ministry of Labour carried out a survey on the characteristics of 84 per cent of the unemployed, a total sample of 219,000. ('Characteristics of the Unemployed', Ministry of Labour, 1962) About 43 per cent of the men had suffered two or more spells of unemployment in the preceding year and a small number as many as eight. About 40 per cent of women had suffered two spells of unemployment and a few three or more. Of the men 28 per cent had held no job in the previous year, 26 per cent two or three jobs and 10 per cent at least four and some more than five. The pattern for women was similar. A considerable number of the unemployed, then, were experiencing frequent job changes and suffering recurring periods of unemployment.

A further survey of the characteristics of the unemployed was carried out by the Department of Employment in 1973. (DE, 1974a) The sample was 16,641. It is interesting to compare the two surveys, given the very different levels of unemployment for the two years. Unemployment in 1961 was just under 300,000; in 1973 it was just over 540,000. In the 1973

survey about 28 per cent of both men and women had suffered two or
more spells of unemployment in the preceding year and 3·5 per cent four
or more. For 70 per cent of the sample, the current spell of
unemployment at the time of the survey was the only spell suffered in the
past year. Compared with the earlier survey, then, in 1973 the incidence
of recurring unemployment had declined. But it had done so at the
expense of longer duration of unemployment. For while in the earlier
survey 'only' 28 per cent of men had held no job in the previous year, by
1973 this was true for 44 per cent of men and 38 per cent of women.

The problem of lengthy duration of unemployment was demonstrated
again in a follow-up survey by the Department of Employment in
January 1974 which produced further evidence on 88 per cent of their
1973 sample. (*ibid.*) Of those men from the 1973 survey, 48 per cent were

TABLE 2.1 *Unemployment by duration. Selected years since 1950*

October	Up to 8 weeks	Over 8 weeks up to 26 weeks	Over 26 weeks up to 52 weeks	Over 52 weeks	Total (000)
1950 *	159·4	52·3	26·3	35·9	273·9
1955 *	113·9	29·4	15·7	21·9	180·9
1960 *	142·8	58·5	35·6	55·3	292·2
1965	158·8	64·6	31·2	51·5	305·7
1970	259·0	143·1	70·2	101·7	574
1971	339·8	238·1	108·1	129·2	815·2
1972	292·8	219·9	116·5	177·6	806·8
1973	198·7	112·9	62·1	142·6	516·3
1974	263·6	159·2	72·0	127·7	622·6
1975	425·3	357·6	154·5	161·2	1098·6
1976	416·7	414·3	225·3	264·6	1320·9

Percentage of total number unemployed					
1950 *	58·2	19·1	9·6	13·1	
1955 *	63·0	16·2	8·7	12·1	
1960 *	48·9	20·0	12·2	18·9	
1965	52·0	21·1	10·2	16·8	
1970	45·1	24·9	12·2	17·7	
1971	41·7	29·2	13·3	15·8	
1972	36·3	27·3	14·4	22·0	
1973	38·5	21·8	12·0	27·6	
1974	42·4	25·6	11·6	20·5	
1975	38·7	32·6	14·1	14·7	
1976	31·5	31·4	17·1	20·0	

* September
The figures for 1975 and 1976 exclude adult students. They are included in
previous years but registration is low in October and was probably non-existent
before the late 1960s. From 1972 casual workers are included.

(*Sources: British Labour Statistics*, 1971; *British Labour Statistics*, 1973, 1976; DE, 1977)

unemployed in January 1974 and only 45 per cent had been employed since the original survey. Recurring unemployment appears then as a serious problem both at times of high and lower unemployment. But when unemployment is at very high levels the problem of recurring unemployment is overtaken by extremely long periods of unemployment for many of the unemployed.

We have seen that analysis of the unemployment flows suggested that a part of the total numbers of unemployed reflects increasing duration of unemployment. Table 2.1 shows that both total unemployment and the duration of unemployment have been increasing steadily since 1950. In October 1950 total unemployment was just over 270,000, and at that time 36,000 people had been unemployed for over a year. By October 1976, total unemployment had reached 1,300,000 and over 260,000 people had been unemployed for over a year.

T.F. Cripps and R.J. Tarling found in their analysis of the duration of male unemployment between 1932 and 1973 that up to a half of those coming onto the register normally leave within two weeks. (Cripps and Tarling, 1974) A similar pattern was found by the Department of Employment. In the early 1950s it was the normal experience for 25 per cent of those unemployed on a given date to have been registered for less than two weeks and for 50 per cent to have been registered for about six weeks; by 1972 the Department found the duration figures had risen to four weeks and fifteen weeks respectively. (DE, 1973a)

The decline in 1974 and 1975 in the percentage of the unemployed suffering unemployment for a year or more might be thought to deny the suggestion that rising unemployment is reflected in increased duration. (Table 2.1) In fact the enormous jump in the numbers unemployed between October 1975 and October 1976 – an increase of over 220,000 – masks the enormous increase in the number of long-term unemployed. Since the total unemployed increased so dramatically in this period, the longest term unemployment, despite having risen by some 180,000 between 1975 and 1976, is a smaller percentage of the unemployed in 1975 and 1976 than in 1974.

What we have seen in 1976 is the beginning of the effects of a high level of unemployment, with the decrease since 1975 of the percentage of unemployed in the two 'shorter' duration periods and an increase in the percentage in the 'higher' duration periods, while for all but the shortest duration numbers have increased. And what we are seeing is the effect of the strong relationship between increases in the numbers of unemployed and increases in the duration of unemployment. How much more serious the problem of long-term unemployment will become as the rapid increase in total unemployment works its way through may not be clear for some time. The indications from the numbers already suffering long periods of unemployment are disheartening.

Who are the unemployed?

In looking at the people affected by unemployment, there is a danger
that the characteristics of the unemployed will, as they do, become
confused with the causes of unemployment. As Adrian Sinfield has
pointed out, the 'acceptance of certain inequalities as "natural" ... has
led scientific research into some odd conclusions'. (Adrian Sinfield, 1976)
If the characteristics of the unemployed are equated with causes,
personal characteristics are stressed while the labour market, macro-
economic and structural forces are devalued or discounted. As J.K.
Bowers and D. Harkess point out,

> it is but a small step to recommend ... the elimination of the long-term
> unemployed and the 'unemployable' however defined, from the
> unemployment statistics ... thereby cutting unemployment
> substantially, making everyone feel better and the economy look
> healthier. (Bowers and Harkess, 1974)

The assumption, for example, from the higher levels of unemployment
experienced by older workers, that it is their age that makes them less
employable, is shown by Sinfield not to be supported by evidence from
other countries. With no implications for causation, then, we turn to
who the unemployed are.

Women and age

It is difficult to give an accurate picture of unemployment among
women because of the extent to which they do not register. What we can
safely say, as a consequence, is that the registered unemployment figures
do understate the amount of unemployment among women. As was
shown in Chapter 1, some idea of the magnitude of this
underregistration is shown in the population census and the General
Household Survey. However, as we can see from Figure 2.1, the evidence
suggests that unemployment among women has been rising fast as a
result of the current recession. Until the end of 1974, men outnumbered
women on the register by five to one; the ratio now is three to one,
perhaps because women are increasingly registering as unemployed.
(Treasury, 1976)

Another way of looking at the increasing unemployment among
women is to compare their share of unemployment with their share of
employment. Employment among women has actually begun to fall
recently, but rose steadily between 1970 and 1976 from 38 per cent to 41
per cent of employees in employment; at the same time female
unemployment has risen from 14 per cent to 25 per cent of total
unemployment – more than trebling in absolute terms. This led the

Annual Report of the Manpower Services Commission to conclude that 'it is clear that female unemployment, though still at a lower level than for males, can no longer be regarded as a minor problem.' (Quoted in *Labour Research*, 1976)

W.W. Daniel has said

the influence of age is overwhelming. It is far more important than jobs in the local labour market, or skill and qualifications. It is much better to be a young worker in an area of high unemployment than an older worker in an area of low unemployment ... if there is one rule it is that, among workers who lose their jobs, the older they are the more difficulty they have in finding a new job, the longer their period out of work, and the more inferior any new job. (Daniel and Stilgoe, 1976)

At almost any level of unemployment it is the older members of the work force who bear the brunt and not simply because of their greater age. Employer preference for the younger worker is not reflected in all other countries by higher unemployment among older workers.

Unless men aged 55 and over in Britain differ in significant characteristics from men of the same age in the United States, Italy or Sweden, or jobs actually require more of an older man in Britain ... we must conclude that there is greater age discrimination in Britain. (Sinfield, 1976, p. 224)

But since the late 1960s the incidence of unemployment has begun to fall heavily on the younger members of the labour force as well. While for both groups their share of unemployment falls as unemployment falls, it is the older members of the work force who continue to bear a disproportionate burden. And, as we shall see later, the older members of the work force are also hit hardest by prolonged unemployment.

In the last ten years men aged 60–64 have accounted for 8 per cent of the labour force; but their unemployment rate has always been at least twice as high and sometimes over 20 per cent. Among the younger age groups, e.g. the under-25s, women have consistently had unemployment rates greater than their share of the labour force. This was not true for men in the 1960s; it is now. In 1972 unemployment for men aged 15–19 was 12 per cent; they were then 7·7 per cent of employees. For the 20–24 years age group the figures were respectively 15 per cent and 11·2 per cent. For women the burden was even greater; 32 per cent of the 15–19 year group were unemployed in 1972 when they were just over 12 per cent of the labour force; for the 20–24 year age group the figures were nearly 23 per cent and 14 per cent. (Mukherjee, 1974, and DE *Gazettes*, August each year) It is well known that older workers are not only more vulnerable than other groups to unemployment but that, once unemployed, their chances of prolonged unemployment are much higher and of getting a job much lower. As Daniel has shown, the chances are that any job they do find will be in some sense inferior to their previous one. (Daniel, 1974)

The figures in Table 2.2 demonstrate, once again, the exceptional burden being placed on the older members of the work force. But concern is now also being expressed about long-term unemployment among the younger age groups and particularly amongst school leavers. It is, after all, as demoralising a way as possible to enter the labour force. In a recent analysis of unemployment among school leavers A.J.H. Dean suggests that there may now be a systematic cumulation of unemployed school leavers from one year to the next. And while it is true that for many school leavers unemployment is only a temporary phenomenon, this is no longer true of other 'teenagers', some of whom in fact may be school leavers. Unemployed school leavers are not classified as such by the Department of Employment if they have reached 18 when they leave school or become unemployed or have held jobs for only a short time before becoming unemployed. (Dean, 1976)

TABLE 2.2 *Unemployment by age and duration. Number and percentage of unemployed in each age group, July 1976*

	Up to 20	20–25	25–55	55–60/65	60/65	Total
			Numbers			
Over 1 mth up to 3 mths	127,109	56,183	133,829	31,614	645	349,380
Over 3 mths up to 6 mths	36,683	43,097	110,923	32,308	558	223,569
Over 6 mths up to 1 year	33,123	42,579	120,181	46,787	816	243,486
Over 1 year	11,092	24,208	116,737	76,373	1,381	229,791
Total : *	390,246	224,850	577,901	205,696	3,783	1,402,470
			% of total			
Over 1 mth up to 3 mths	32·6	25·0	23·2	15·4	17·0	24·9
Over 3 mths up to 6 mths	9·4	19·2	19·2	15·7	14·8	15·9
Over 6 mths up to 1 year	8·5	18·9	20·8	22·7	21·6	17·4
Over 1 year	2·8	10·8	20·2	37·1	36·5	16·4
Total % : †	53·3	73·9	83·4	90·9	89·9	74·6

*Of all durations.
† All unemployed one month or more as a per cent of total unemployed. Excludes persons temporarily stopped and adult students.

(*Source*: DE, 1976c)

While the problems of school leavers and young people facing unemployment are undoubtedly very serious, they fared better between 1963 and 1973 than the older members of the work force. J.K. Bowers has shown that, unlike older workers, their expected duration of unemployment, while fluctuating, has not been on a markedly rising trend. But for both men and women over 55 years changes in expected duration have been on a markedly rising trend. Over the ten years from 1963 expected duration for women rose by four weeks to twenty weeks; for men by seven weeks to just over 30 weeks. (Table 2.3)

TABLE 2.3 *Unemployment duration: expected duration in weeks, July each year.*

	Age 16 – 18		Age 18 – 25		Age 55 +	
	Women	Men	Women	Men	Women	Men
1963	2·8	3·2	6·7	4·8	16·0	24·5
1964	2·4	2·5	5·2	3·5	13·0	22·6
1965	1·7	1·8	4·5	3·0	11·6	22·8
1966	2·0	2·2	3·8	2·8	10·9	21·8
1967	2·7	2·8	5·4	5·1	15·1	25·9
1968	2·3	2·6	4·8	5·2	14·5	27·4
1969	2·4	2·6	4·5	4·8	14·9	30·1
1970	2·7	3·0	4·9	5·0	18·1	31·6
1971	3·5	4·0	5·6	6·7	20·8	34·1
1972	3·9	4·4	5·8	7·1	22·2	36·0
1973	3·2	3·3	4·2	4·7	20·1	31·4

(*Source*: Bowers and Harkess, 1976)

Age is a powerful factor influencing vulnerability to both unemployment and to long-term unemployment. It is above all the older worker who suffers. But we should be aware too of the plight of the young and school leavers starting and possibly spending some considerable amount of their early working lives unemployed. Nor should we forget that as unemployment rises, more people of all ages are suffering unemployment and for longer periods and that those in the generally least affected groups and their dependants are also sharing the burden.

Occupation and disability

Sinfield has commented that: 'The unequal incidence of unemployment by occupation is one of those facts about society so well known that it is rarely discussed.' (Sinfield, 1976, p. 222). The lack of hard evidence on the demand for and availability of various types of skills in the labour force is commonly bemoaned; but there is no lack of evidence on who suffers the greatest unemployment. It is the unskilled and increasingly so. In 1974 Mukherjee concluded 'the evidence seems to point to there being a persistent oversupply of unskilled labour in relation to the demand for that kind of manpower. That proposition holds good, but to a lesser extent, even when the economy is booming.' (Mukherjee, 1974)

The unskilled have always borne a disproportionate share of unemployment. Sinfield has estimated that since 1959, when occupational data for the unemployed were first published, over half of the unemployed men, and sometimes more, have been registered as labourers, the general category for the unskilled. The contrast with skilled workers, as Mukherjee emphasises, is marked: 'no matter how hard the times are, demand does not fall in the market to an extent comparable to the decline which occurs for unskilled labour'.

An analysis by the Department of Employment for 1959 to 1972 reached similar conclusions. In September of each of four selected years, 1959, 1963, 1968 and 1972, the 'main labouring occupations' had consistently represented over 50 per cent of total unemployment despite the change in total unemployment from just over 250,000 in 1959 to 650,000 in 1972. (DE, 1973b) A sample survey by the Department in June 1973 again demonstrated the disadvantaged position of the unskilled, 'general labourers' forming half the unemployed. But the most striking contrast with the unemployed in general that the survey revealed, was the length of time the unskilled had been out of work. About 40 per cent of the 'general labourers' had been out of work for over a year, compared with about 25 per cent of the remainder of the unemployed. (DE, 1974b)

Other surveys have added to the weight of this evidence. In the 1971 General Household Survey, 27 per cent of the economically active population were classified as unskilled or semi-skilled manual workers; 42 per cent of the unemployed in the GHS sample were in this category and in the 1973 PEP survey, 54 per cent. (Daniel, 1974) At the other end of the scale, 44 per cent of the economically active population were non-manual workers with unemployment rates of 25 per cent (GHS) and 22 per cent (PEP). Both skilled and supervisory workers had unemployment rates equal to their proportions of the economically active population.

The substantial rise in unemployment since 1974 has had the effect of reducing the percentage rate of unemployment for the unskilled as other occupational groups have begun to experience higher levels of unemployment. In September 1976, 'general labourers' accounted for 36 per cent of total unemployment; in September 1975 they had been 42 per cent. But as we can see from Figure 2.2, in 1976 with 434,605 'general labourers' unemployed, they still accounted for the largest share of the unemployed.

Perhaps even more illuminating of the disadvantaged position of the unemployed once out of a job is the number of job opportunities. However, in comparing 'notified vacancies' and 'registered unemployed' one needs to remember that as the latter understates the level of unemployment, so the former may understate the number of

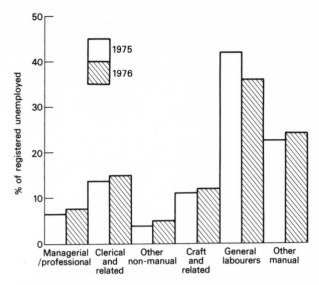

(*Sources*: DE, 1975b, DE, 1976e)

FIGURE 2.2 *Occupational analysis of the unemployed*

vacancies available. None the less the comparison is important. Sinfield has calculated that in the fifteen years between 1959 and 1974 there was at best one vacancy for every four unemployed labourers. In 1974 the ratio was one to three compared with 1 to 1·5 for all other occupations. (Sinfield, 1976, p. 222) In September 1975 the ratio of unemployed 'general labourers' to notified vacancies was 70 to 1; in 1976 56 to 1. In terms of vacancies, by the end of 1976, general labourers were almost ten times worse off than all other groups.

That 'general labourers' have declined as a proportion of the total unemployed is merely a reflection of the fact that at very high levels of unemployment other occupational groups are beginning to feel the effects as well. But while all occupational groups are now feeling the effects of the exceptionally high levels of unemployment, it is, as it has always has been, the least skilled members of the work force who are bearing the brunt.

Another group bearing the burden of unemployment is the disabled. Like other vulnerable groups their share of unemployment is far in excess of the general level of unemployment and as unemployment worsens, so does their proportion of it. In October 1976 there were 76,545 disabled people registered as unemployed (who were also registered under the Disabled Persons (Employment) Acts, 1944 and 1958). (DE, 1976g) Of this number, 76 per cent were considered suitable for ordinary employment. Unemployment among the registered disabled has been rising steadily over the last two years from 11·3 per cent in February 1975 to 14·1 per cent in October 1976, the most recently available figure. (*Hansard*, 1977j; col. 299)

Regional differences

'For as long as there has been an interest in the regional problems in this country, there has been concern over the differences in unemployment between regions. Unemployment differences have almost been *the* regional problem.' (Cheshire, 1973). Three regions have consistently suffered higher levels of unemployment – the North, Scotland and Wales – and have done so for the past fifty years. They have at times had unemployment rates three times as high as the lowest regional rate.

The regional unemployment rates show that all the regions have been affected by rising unemployment. In 1965 regional unemployment rates ranged from 0·7 per cent to 2·9 per cent; in 1975 the range was 2·9 per cent to 6·3 per cent. Since 1972, however, divergences between regional unemployment rates have narrowed (as tends to occur when unemployment is rising). (DE, 1974b) This can be seen by looking at the ratio of regional unemployment to national unemployment. In 1965 the rates ranged from 0·5 to 2·1; in 1975 from 0·7 to 1·5. But despite the narrowing of the unemployment rates, the North, Scotland and Wales are still suffering the highest unemployment rates – as they were ten, and indeed twenty, years ago. With unemployment rates in 1975 of 5·3 per cent in Scotland, 6 per cent in Wales and 6·3 per cent in the North, the comparison with the average Great Britain rate of 4·3 per cent and the lowest regional rate in the country of 2·9 per cent in the South-East, speaks for itself. It is not only for the regions that the national figures mask the incidence of unemployment; the same is true for the development regions within them and for the inner cities. The figures in Table 2.4 show that, despite their designated government aid, they continue to experience higher levels of unemployment than their corresponding regions.

There is also considerable difference between the regions in the duration of unemployment. The figures show that, in general, the regions which have suffered the highest unemployment in the past ten years or so have also seen the longest duration periods for men. However, the effect of a substantially higher unemployment rate in 1972 (and rising unemployment since 1970) seems to have slightly altered the relative fortunes of the regions. By 1970 the median duration for men in the East Midlands was higher than in Scotland, traditionally one of the three hardest hit areas. By 1972 equally high duration rates were being suffered in the East Midlands and in Yorkshire and Humberside. But the

TABLE 2.4 *Development Areas and Special Development Areas*

	% unemployed	
	August 1975	August 1976
South-West	7·8	9·5
Merseyside (SDA)	10·6	11·5
N. Yorkshire	4·5	5·4
Northern	7·9	8·7
North-East (SDA)	8·8	9·6
W. Cumberland (SDA)	8·2	9·1
Scottish	6·3	7·9
Scottish (SDA's)	7·4	9·3
Wales	7·5	8·2
Welsh (SDA's)	9·8	10·7
Great Britain	4·8	6·3

Adult students are included in 1975 but not in 1976

(*Source*: DE, 1975a, 1976d)

Department of Employment surveys in 1973 and 1974 again showed the contrast between the regions: while 20 per cent of unemployed men in the South-East had been unemployed for over a year, in no other region was this true for less than 30 per cent of men and in some areas it was as high as 38 per cent. ('Characteristics of the unemployed: analysis by region', DE, 1974c)

Certain regions, then, have consistently experienced higher rates of unemployment; to live in certain areas is to run a higher risk of unemployment than in others. It is only now, when we have been experiencing rapid increases in the level of unemployment and sustained exceptionally high levels, that we are beginning to see a change in the relative positions of the regions.

Racial disadvantage in unemployment

Unemployment among racial minority groups is characterised by two outstanding features; their vulnerability in periods of rising and high unemployment and the generally higher levels of unemployment among the young and women from racial minorities at all levels of unemployment. These unemployment experiences of the racial minorities have been extensively documented in a recent PEP survey; we have drawn heavily on their data.

Since the early 1960s the unemployment of racial minorities compared to the general population can be divided into two contrasting periods. Until 1970 unemployment was higher for the minority groups than for the general population although, apart from 1966–8, the gap was gradually narrowing. In 1963 for example, unemployment among minority groups was about four times as high as the general level of unemployment. These higher levels were probably due to the effects of a high level of immigration in the early 1960s.

Between 1970 and 1974, on the other hand, the minorities have had similar rates of unemployment to the general population. Using Department of Employment data, the PEP survey calculated the average unemployment among minorities between 1971 and 1975 to have been 2·5 per cent of the unemployed, with their own survey suggesting that this approximated to the minorities' percentage share of the work force in the 1970s.

But their experience of unemployment since 1974 seems to have worsened as unemployment has risen. Between 1973 and 1975 the increase for minority workers was nearly two-and-a-half times that of the unemployed generally.(DE,1976d, Table I, p. 868) The Department of Employment suggested that a part of this greater vulnerability is explained by the younger age structure of the minority population; the rise in unemployment among the under-25s generally was particularly marked during 1974 and the beginning of 1975. However, that unemployment among minority groups increases as a proportion of unemployment when unemployment is rising supports the theory that minority groups' workers function as a marginal source of labour and are more vulnerable to unemployment when its impact is greatest. (Smith, 1976)

Women and young people from minority groups

Unlike the minority population in general, women and young people from minority groups have consistently had unemployment rates higher than their general populations.

Figures from the 1971 census (which are not distorted by the tendency of women not to register as unemployed) show that unemployment among women from minority groups was 9·3 per cent in that year compared to 5·6 per cent for women in general. Unemployment has been particularly marked among younger women. Unemployment rates have also been particularly high among young male West Indians. In 1971, the census figures show 16·9 per cent of young West Indian males as unemployed, twice the rate for other young economically active males, at 8·6 per cent. The high incidence of unemployment among young West Indians has been well documented elsewhere. Concern about these high levels is increased by the extent to which the official Department of Employment figures may underestimate unemployment because of non-registration. A CRC survey in 1972 suggested that about 50 per cent of the young unemployed were not registered. (Community

Relations Commission, 1974, Table 12, p.68). There is also evidence to suggest that minority workers in employment have lower jobs in socio-economic terms, than the general population given similar educational levels, and that the educational level of the unemployed is surprisingly high. Racial minorities are also overrepresented in non-skilled manual jobs; given the low ratio of vacancies to the unemployed amongst this skill group, the minorities are once again at a disadvantage.

Conclusion

We have looked in this chapter at who the unemployed are and where they are. We have seen how vulnerability to unemployment varies and, far from falling like God's gentle rain, it 'strikes from underneath and strikes particularly hard at those at the bottom of society'. (Liebow, 1970) And we have seen how the disadvantaged position of some groups in society is increased when unemployment is rising and when, as now, it is at extremely high levels. Although, even when unemployment is high there are still large numbers of people leaving the register each week, none the less more people are becoming unemployed and they are remaining unemployed for longer. Another consequence of rising unemployment and a rapidly changing register is the tendency for people to be faced with the prospect of unemployment punctuated by short periods of employment. But more recently we have seen that, while recurring unemployment seems to have lessened, it has done so only at the expense of longer stretches of unemployment punctuated by employment.

Faced with the highest level of unemployment since the 1930s, those who fare worse than most in the labour market in the fight for jobs have become doubly disadvantaged. We have seen how certain areas and certain groups, for example, the unskilled, older workers, and racial minorities are shouldering the greater part of the burden. But an analysis of the composition of the unemployed has also shown that at these high levels of unemployment, while the same section of the work force is continuing to bear the brunt, other sections, traditionally unaffected by unemployment, are beginning to feel its effects.

3   Unemployment and poverty

Frank Field

Powerful arguments are put forward in support of running the economy at a higher level of unemployment as a cure for inflation or balance-of-payments problems. Those who believe this also allege that the hardship created is alleviated by a generous welfare state. It is also argued that the more generous provision of welfare benefits has itself been a cause in the rise in the number of jobless, as some people now prefer to be unemployed and draw benefit than resume full-time work. In this chapter we analyse the truth behind these arguments. In the first place we look at the range of benefits available to the unemployed and examine their effectiveness in preventing poverty. In the second half of the chapter we turn to the argument that the provision of redundancy payments, the introduction of the earnings-related supplement scheme to flat-rate unemployment pay, more generous benefits together with tax refunds now make it financially more advantageous for a considerable number of people to remain idle for at least part of the year.

Benefits for the unemployed

There are three benefits for the unemployed; the flat-rate unemployment benefit, the earnings-related supplement and supplementary benefit. In addition a worker may qualify under the redundancy payment scheme. However, this is a payment to compensate him for loss of his job, rather than to tide him over the period during which he is out of work.

People who work for an employer are usually covered by unemployment benefit after the first three days of unemployment; the self-employed are excluded from this scheme. In order to qualify for unemployment benefit a claimant has to satisfy the contributions conditions and show that he is available for work.

An unemployed claimant may draw flat-rate unemployment benefit for up to 312 days and, as Sundays are not included as payment days, this amounts to twelve months in any one period of interruption of employment. Once a claimant has exhausted his right to benefit he cannot qualify again for unemployment benefit until he has been back at work and paying contributions as an employed person for at least thirteen weeks. The rates for flat-rate unemployment benefit are shown in Table 3.1.

TABLE 3.1 *Unemployment pay, November 1976*

	Weekly rate (£)
Higher rate	12·90
Increase for wife or other adult dependent	8·00
Increase for children:	
First child	4·05
Second child*	2·55
Any other child*	2·55

* Child benefits bring the total payments up to the amount payable for the first child.

A claimant may be eligible for an earnings-related supplement to his flat-rate unemployment benefit if he is aged 18 and over and under minimum pensionable age. This benefit entitlement runs for six months. There are, however, three main conditions for entitlement. The first is that the claimant must be receiving flat-rate unemployment benefit. The second is that he must have 'reckonable earnings' of at least £550 in the relevant tax year. And third, he must have completed twelve waiting days, i.e. the claimant must have been registered at the employment exchange for twelve working days unless he was registered for work or was ill during the previous thirteen weeks, when the spells are lumped together.

Earnings-related supplement is paid according to the claimant's average weekly earnings in the relevant tax year. In the tax year 1975–6 this was between £11 and £69. The supplement payable is approximately one third of the amount by which a claimant's average earnings exceeded £11 a week up to £30, plus 15 per cent of the income from £30 up to £69.

Although claimants will have paid their full contributions, they are disallowed from drawing a full earnings-related supplement if, together with the flat-rate benefit, this brings their total benefit to above 85 per cent of their average weekly earnings. Even the official definition of average weekly earnings works against many low paid, for these are not their current weekly earnings. Instead, a claimant's total reckonable earnings in the relevant tax year are divided by fifty and this sum can often be considerably lower than current earnings. The relevant tax year refers to the last completed financial year prior to the claim for benefit. So a claim in December 1977 will be based on earnings during the tax

year April 1975 to April 1976. In Table 3.2 we give examples of the extent
of help offered under the earnings-related benefit scheme for claimants
on different levels of income. The table also gives information on how
the weekly benefit ceiling operates to ensure that claimants do not draw
in benefit more than 85 per cent of their average weekly earnings.
During 1976, 61,800 unemployed claimants had this 'wage stop' imposed
on their benefit even though they had paid the contributions for a full
earnings-related benefit. (*Hansard*, 1976p, col. 1442)

TABLE 3.2 *Examples of earnings-related benefit payable at January 1977, based
(ERB) on earnings in the 1975–6 tax year*

Annual reckonable earnings	Weekly ERBs rate	Weekly benefit ceiling
£	£	£
551	0·01	9·37
1,000	3·00	17·00
2,010	7·86	34·17
3,000	10·83	51·26
3,450	12·18	58·65

An unemployed man and his family may also be eligible for
supplementary benefit. The supplementary benefit scheme's main
purpose is to ensure that the income of people who are unable to work
does not fall below a minimum level set by Parliament. Unemployed
claimants and their families who have few private resources on which to
fall back may be eligible for a weekly payment from the Supplementary
Benefit Commission to bring their unemployment and earnings-related
benefit up to the state poverty line. In the case of unemployed claimants
this is the ordinary scale rate and Table 3.3 gives this information.
Unemployed claimants who are the head of the household are also
eligible for a payment which covers their weekly rent and rates.

Stigmatising the unemployed

A major distinction is made between claimants who, it is alleged, are
long-term beneficiaries and those who, it is deemed, draw benefit for
only a short period of time. Underlying this distinction is a belief that
unemployment is, by its very nature, only of short-term duration (and
the unemployed can therefore draw a national insurance benefit for up
to a maximum of one year). As a result, those claimants who are old or
widowed draw a higher rate of national insurance benefit. Long-term

TABLE 3.3 *Supplementary benefit rates from November 1976*

	Ordinary rate	Long-term rate
	£	£
Husband and wife	20·65	24·85
Person living alone	12·70	15·70
Any other person aged:		
Not less than 18	10·15	12·60
Less than 18 but not less than 16	7·80	—
Less than 16 but not less than 13	6·50	—
Less than 13 but not less than 11	5·35	—
Less than 11 but not less than 5	4·35	—
Less than 5	3·60	—

single claimants draw a weekly benefit of £15.30 as opposed to £12.90 if they are sick or unemployed, and £24.50 as a married couple, compared with £20.90 for those claimants who are classified as short-term beneficiaries. The rate for children also vary. The first children of claimants on the higher rate attract a weekly benefit of £7.45, with payments of £5.95 for second and subsequent children in contrast to weekly allowances of £4.05 for the first and £2.55 for the other children of sick or unemployed claimants.

There is a similar distinction between so-called long- and short-term claimants in the supplementary benefit scheme. Ever since 1966, when the Ministry of Social Security Act came into force, there has been a tiered system of benefits. All pensioners in receipt of supplementary benefit, together with those below pensionable age who are not required to register for work and have been drawing benefit for two or more years, were automatically awarded an additional 45p a week. By 1972 this sum had been increased to 60p a week. In October 1973, with the introduction of what is called the long-term scale rate, the difference rose to £1.20 for a couple, £1 for a single householder and 90p for a single non-householder. When the new supplementary benefit rates became effective in November 1976 the difference between those on the long-term scale rate and other claimants rose to £4.20 a week for couples, £3.00 for single persons and £2.45 for non-householders.

The reasoning behind the long- and short-term scale rates is sound. Claimants who have been on benefit for any length of time are likely to have exhausted their savings and to be experiencing a severe depletion of household stocks, such as bedding, furniture, clothing and so on. What is wrong is that the distinction is misapplied for, as we have seen in Chapter 2, a growing number of unemployed are also long-term claimants. As the unemployed are automatically excluded from the long-term rate, irrespective of the time they have been on benefit, the rule helps to reinforce in the public eye the false distinction between 'deserving' and 'undeserving' claimants.

The distinction between the long- and short-term claimants has a legislative base in the various social security acts. However, the SBC has wide discretionary powers. Not only can it deny a claimant benefit at a moment's notice, but it can add regular weekly additions to a claimant's benefit (ECA) or a lump sum payment (ENP). How do the unemployed fare in winning these discretionary additions? To answer this question we examine the comparisons the DHSS made of the circumstances of families on supplementary benefits. (Marshall, 1972)

The study showed that 29 per cent of unemployed families surveyed – a higher percentage than of any other group – specified that they needed no furniture or household equipment at present, but a careful analysis shows that they were not nearly so favourably placed with respect to clothing and bedding. For example, 29 per cent of the unemployed men claimed that their families had insufficient blankets for the winter, and 48 per cent possessed stocks of less than three sheets per bed. Similarly, 51 per cent of the unemployed men in the survey stated that their children had secondhand shoes. This compared with the 44 per cent of unmarried mothers, 36 per cent of separated wives, 30 per cent of claimants who were sick, 30 per cent of divorced women and 19 per cent of widows.

The study examined the award of exceptional needs payments in relation to each family's 'basic need'; the basic need being defined as the supplementary benefit level. Families were then divided into those who had an income greater than their basic needs and those with an income equal to or less than their basic needs. Families were then further classified according to whether the head of the household was unemployed, sick or a single-parent family. The results of this analysis showed that of those families receiving an ENP in the previous twelve months who were headed by a claimant who was sick or a lone parent, the vast majority had incomes greater than their basic needs. On the other hand, few unemployed claimants and their families received an ENP if their income was greater than the supplementary benefit level. (*ibid.*, Table 57, p. 47, Table b.6)

No unemployed claimants and their families were eligible for long-term additions. However, 29 per cent of families headed by a claimant who was sick compared with 32 per cent headed by a wife separated from her husband, 38 per cent of unmarried mothers, 64 per cent of divorced mothers and 48 per cent of widows received the long-term addition, as it was then called. But whereas the unemployed are automatically excluded from the long-term scale rate, the same does not automatically apply for ECAs. Nevertheless, of all the different family groups studied, unemployed men and their families are least likely to be awarded an ECA. (*ibid.*, Table d.7)

Unemployment and poverty

Despite the provisions of the national insurance scheme, an increasing number of unemployed claimants are being plunged into poverty. This can be seen from Figure 3.1, which shows the numbers of unemployed resorting to the SBC in order to bring their income up to the state poverty line. But why is it that, with the provision of social security measures which, in Beveridge's phrase, were designed to prevent want being the inevitable result of unemployment, we find an increasing pauperisation amongst the unemployed?

There are two reasons why the present national insurance scheme does not prevent poverty resulting from unemployment. The first is that not every unemployed person is covered by the scheme because either they have insufficient contributions, or they have been unemployed for a long time and have therefore exhausted their right to unemployment benefit. The second reason is that in most instances unemployment benefit is not paid at a level high enough to raise the income of those claimants who have no private resources to a level above the state poverty lines. We now examine the importance of both of these causes in turn.

The government regularly publishes data on the numbers of unemployed and the type of benefit to which they are entitled. The latest detailed breakdown of these figures is reproduced in Table 3.4. From this it emerges that at any one time one in six claimants is drawing no benefit at all. As we have already explained in Chapter 2, most of the information presented by the Department is a snapshot of the unemployed. Valuable as this is, it does not however tell us the whole story. Some of those claimants who were found to be drawing no benefit at all on the day of the count were in the process of registering their claim for benefit. The DHSS has explained that about a quarter of those drawing no benefit on the day of the count will in due course be found to have been entitled to unemployment benefit for the day of the count.

> In addition, some will qualify for unemployment benefit for later days, when they have completed their waiting days for benefit or when the disqualification expires, and others will qualify for supplementary benefit when they have exhausted their immediate resources, usually their last wages. (*Hansard*, 1975b, col. 215)

This explanation does not account for the majority of those who, on the day of the count, are found to be drawing no benefit whatsoever. It is true some of these claimants may be retired white-collar workers between the ages of 60 and 65 who register at the employment exchange so they can be credited with contributions towards their national insurance pension. However, other evidence published by the government draws attention to the large numbers of unemployed men

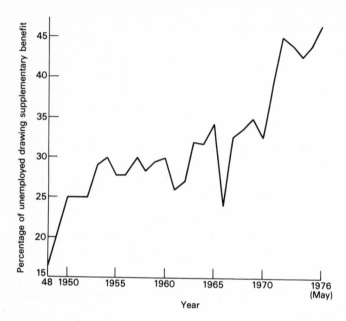

FIGURE 3.1 *Growth in the numbers of unemployed drawing supplementary benefit, 1948–76*

and their families living on incomes below the state poverty line. Data released for December 1972 showed that there were 120,000 households containing 190,000 persons where the breadwinner had been unemployed for more than three months, whose income was below the current supplementary benefit level but who were not claiming supplementary benefit. By reworking these data Adrian Sinfield illustrates the fact that more than half of those unemployed for more than three months and not receiving supplementary allowance were living on incomes below the supplementary benefit level. Expressing this another way, Sinfield concludes that for every two unemployed persons receiving supplementary benefit there was one person eligible but not receiving benefit. (Sinfield, 1974)

Not only are a minority of unemployed claimants drawing national insurance benefits, but the proportion has been falling in recent years; from over 70 per cent in 1948 to less than 40 per cent in 1976. Details of this trend are presented in Figure 3.2. But even if a claimant is eligible for the flat-rate unemployment pay, this will not automatically raise his income to a level above the state poverty line. For example, if a claimant has two children aged 7 and 12 and pays rent of £5 a week, the poverty line income for himself and his family is £31.10 a week. His flat-rate

TABLE 3.4 *Unemployed persons registered on 3 May 1976, analysed by benefit entitlement*

	All persons	Total	Flat rate payable (000)					
			Flat rate benefit only	Flat rate benefit and ERS	Flat rate benefit, ERS and supplementry allowance	Flat rate benefit and supplementry allowance	Supplementary allowance only	No flat rate or supplementry allowance
Males	952	468	167	174	27	100	399	145
Females	248	120	66	40	4	10	73	55
Total:	1,200	588	233	214	31	110	412	200

(*Source*: Hansard, 1977b, cols 357–8, 4 per cent sample)

unemployment benefit, however, comes to only £27.50.

As we have seen, the claimant may be eligible for earnings-related benefit. Although this can provide an important additional source of income for unemployed men and their families, wage-related payments do not automatically guarantee that a family will have an income above the state poverty line. In May 1976 there were 31,000 claimants drawing flat-rate unemployment benefit plus earnings-related supplement who also qualified for a supplementary allowance. What we do not know, however, is the number of unemployed men drawing flat-rate and wage-related unemployment benefit whose income was below the state poverty line but, through ignorance of their rights or for some other reason, failed to claim supplementary allowance.

Because of our failure to provide a comprehensive and generous income support system we have seen that losing one's job is still a major cause of poverty in this country. Given the current economic forecast and ministers' predictions, it appears that unemployment is likely to become a more common cause of poverty during the next few years. Just how significant a cause of family poverty can be seen from Table 3.5, which looks at the growth in the numbers of unemployed drawing supplementary benefits and expresses these totals for the different years as a percentage of all beneficiaries below pensionable age dependent on supplementary allowances. During 1977 unemployment had once again become the single most important reason why families were pushed into poverty.

Voluntary unemployment

Given this information on the poverty which accompanies long-term

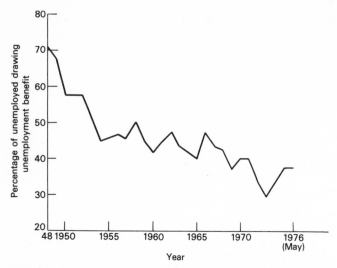

FIGURE 3.2 *Percentage of unemployed claimants drawing only flat rate national insurance benefit, 1948–76*

unemployment, critics have begun to change tack. The spectre now being raised is one of short-term voluntary unemployment due to the provision of redundancy payments, earnings-related supplements and tax rebates. The charge is that the network of benefits and rebates makes large numbers of workers financially better off not working for part of the year. This campaign then begins developing along more familiar lines. As people are opting for voluntary unemployment, the government should relax in the face of higher unemployment. In the remainder of this chapter we examine more fully this theory concerning a rise in voluntary unemployment, before reviewing evidence of what actually happens in practice.

David Metcalfe and Ray Richardson have expressed this view in the following terms.

> When the government raises unemployment compensation, introduces earnings related unemployment compensation, extends redundancy payment schemes, and increases the subsidy to training schemes, one would expect to observe a rise in the number of single people not at work, i.e. not producing in the current period. At least some of the rise in unemployment observed after 1965 should be ascribed to such policies. (Metcalfe and Richardson, 1972, p. 39).

However, these two writers have also observed that, despite the evidence we have drawn upon earlier in this chapter, 'the social policies and the unemployment they cause do not imply hardship and do not necessarily

TABLE 3.5 *The numbers and percentage of unemployed supplementary benefit claimants*

Year	Number (000s)	Percentage of all allowance cases
1960	128	24·6
1961	131	24·6
1962	202	31·8
1963	185	28·9
1964	131	22·7
1965	112	19·4
1966	179	26·5
1967	224	29·7
1968	220	28·3
1969	228	28·0
1970	239	28·6
1971	387	39·1
1972	392	39·1
1973	249	30·0
1974	301	34·5
1975	541	48·6
1976*	603	50·6

* May

(*Source*: *Hansard*, 1977l, col. 64)

imply waste.' (*ibid.*, p. 41) They also lend weight to an 'extremely tentative' measure of the extent to which the social security reforms have resulted in increased unemployment. The increase in the value of flat-rate unemployment pay together with the addition of earnings-related benefits have resulted in 'perhaps a 25 per cent increase in unemployment as officially measured.' (*ibid.*, p. 40)

Sam Brittan has made a similar point. He maintains that three forces are at work which have increased the numbers of voluntary unemployed. First has been the introduction of redundancy payments in December 1965 and the earnings-related supplement scheme in October 1966. 'These extra benefits make it easier for the unemployed worker to spend longer searching for a good job offer than before, and this increased search activity may well be socially desirable, despite the effects on the unemployment totals.' (Brittan, 1976, p. 254) Second, 'At least as important has probably been the increase in standard social security benefits. This could help to explain the increase in medium and long term jobless, who are unlikely to be affected by any form of severance pay.' (*ibid.*, p. 255) In support of this argument Sam Brittan recalls that the supplementary benefit level for a three-child family in 1967–70 was estimated at 68 per cent of net average male manual earnings, commenting that this represents 'a notable increase' compared with 1954–60, when the payment to an equivalent unemployed family represented 55 per cent of average earnings. And again Sam Brittan adds a comment which, it must be said, is consistent with his approach to this subject: 'the improvements were thoroughly justified, but it would be contrary to all experience if this did not reduce initiative to seek work of those with limited earning prospects.' (*ibid.*, p. 255)

The National Institute of Economic and Social Research recently considered the validity of the widely held view of a narrowing gap between the incomes of an unemployed person and one on average earnings. A comparison was made of the income of adult male workers in full-time employment after they had paid tax and received any benefits to which they are entitled for the years from 1967 to 1976. This information was then compared with a 'representative' family with an unemployed head of the household. For the purposes of the example the family's income was made up from flat-rate and earnings-related benefit for unemployed claimants. In other words the illustration assumes that claimants are drawing the most favourable combination of benefits, whereas we have already seen that only a small minority are found to be entitled at any one time.

These two sets of data were then expressed as a ratio of benefits to disposable and net earnings. In April 1967 the ratio was 66. In the following year it rose to 71. In no year since then has the ratio risen above 70 and in 1976 it had fallen to 65 per cent. From this the National Institute concluded 'the impression is that there has been little change in the net benefit earnings ratio in recent years'. (NIESR, 1977, p. 60)

The third force allegedly at work 'has probably been the increase in involvement of manual workers with a cumulative PAYE system, which provides a cushion of repayments for those who lose or leave their jobs'. (Brittan, 1976, p. 256) More recently this argument has been developed in an attempt to show that practically half the labour force are better off out of work than when following their normal occupation. What evidence is there to support these allegations?

W.W. Daniel, drawing on a national sample of unemployed claimants in 1973, was anxious to find out whether the level of welfare provision prevented workers from returning to work. He found that

> There was no general indication that the current level of social benefits was discouraging workers from wanting to return to work. The overwhelming weight of evidence pointed to the conclusion that it was the physical, social and psychological characteristics of workers: their age, stage in the life cycle, number of dependants, strength, state of health, and level in society when working that determined how keen

they were to work, and that the level of social benefits played a very small part in the overall picture.

Indeed, paradoxically for those who argue that more generous welfare benefits have increased the numbers of voluntarily unemployed, the national survey results showed that 'the more unemployed workers were receiving in social benefits, the more concerned they were about being out of work'. (Daniel, 1974, p. 151) More important, Daniels found that it was the level of pay in their last employment which played a more decisive part in determining a worker's attitude to employment opportunities. (*ibid.*, p. 152) Higher-paid workers were found to be more willing to accept reductions in money earnings than were lower-paid workers. 'Those who had earned less than £20 in their last job gave figures suggesting that they would not be prepared to accept a new job unless it paid 20 per cent more in money than the one they had lost.' But if account is taken of the time claimants have been unemployed and the rate of inflation, 'they would have needed an increase of that level to stand still'. (*ibid.*, 152) The survey also highlighted the fact that the tendency of the very low paid to expect increases in earnings before rejoining the labour force was 'largely determined by the very large proportion of women in this category, who may have had special reasons associated with their domestic circumstances for needing extra to make it worth their while [to return to work].' (*ibid.*, 152)

In analysing the most common reasons given by the unemployed workers in Woolwich for turning down jobs it was found that the most important reason was related to the low rate of pay (42 per cent), that the work was not suited to the claimant's skills or training (the reason given by 22 per cent) and third, that the job was too far away from home. 'Only 3 per cent said that the reason they turned jobs down was because they were offered less than they were getting in social benefits.' (Daniel, 1972, p. 99)

We have already seen that some writers have alleged that the introduction of the redundancy-payment scheme has also had the effect of increasing the numbers of voluntarily unemployed. Two surveys are to hand as well as data published by the government which help us to look more carefully at this hypothesis. From this latter source it can be seen that only a minority of unemployed workers receive payments under the scheme. The latest information shows that, during 1975, 340,215 employees qualified under the scheme and, on average, received a payment of £524 (*Hansard*, 1977b, cols 373–4) During the same year, 4,400,000 claimants registered as unemployed. On average, then, 7 per cent of the unemployed received payments under the scheme.

That redundancy payments affect only a small minority of the unemployed emerges from the national survey of the unemployed. Of

those surveyed in 1973 (when unemployment was at about one third of
the present level) only 7 per cent had received payments under the
Redundancy Payments Act on leaving their last job and 'these tended to
be among the higher occupational levels'. (Daniel, 1974, p. 153) But for
those who received help under this scheme, did these payments have any
effect in lessening their wish to return to work? A detailed study of
workers made redundant in the Woolwich area of London helps to
answer this question. Here it was found that

> there was no tendency ... for the size of the lump sum payments to be
> associated with the delaying of job seeking. In particular, there was no
> consistent trend for those who had not found a job prior to dismissal to
> 'wait a while' before looking for a job, the higher their lump sum
> payments. (Daniel, 1972, p. 99)

As the report notes

> these findings are a more effective test and refutation of the idea that
> redundancy payments prolong periods of unemployment
> unnecessarily, than is the length of time they actually took to find a
> job, because the time at which they initiated job seeking was largely in
> their own hands but the time at which they found a job depended not
> only on their own efforts, but the extent to which there were suitable
> jobs open to them and they were acceptable to employers, which
> introduces factors outside their control. (*ibid.*, p. 100)

The third strand in this argument alleges that considerable numbers of
workers are better off not working than they are gainfully employed.
What is the truth of this allegation? We draw on two sources of
information. The first brings together the findings from surveys of the
unemployed. The second looks at the views of officers in the DE about
the wage levels which unemployed workers can expect when they are
offered a job.

The survey of unemployed men in three English towns reported:
'There seems to be no evidence from this survey to substantiate the view
that many men remain unemployed because it is more lucrative than
working. It is very doubtful that more than a very small number of men
fall into this category.' This research pinpointed the fact that 'it cannot
be conclusively proved that longer periods of unemployment are due to
high unemployment income, rather than the possession of other
characteristics such as a low level of skill.' (Hill, Harrison, Sargeant and
Talbot, 1973, p. 130)

The national survey supports this view although it does record 'a
minority, however, who were receiving more in benefit income than
they had in their last job.' (Daniel, 1974, p. 115) Of those who had been
getting £15 or less from their former job 13 per cent had been receiving

more than £15 in benefit. Of those who had been earning over £15 to £20 in their last job 6 per cent had been receiving over £20 in benefit and 1 per cent of those who had earned over £20 to £25 and those earning £25 to £30 in work had been receiving over £25 and over £30 respectively in benefit.

However, even these figures, small as they are, need to be viewed with some caution. Since current levels of benefit were being compared with previous earnings a more accurate means of judging whether claimants are better off not working is to examine the levels of reward they could currently draw if they were able to move back into the labour market. Unfortunately, this is not a question any of the surveys on the unemployed attempted to ask. However, the DE has analysed those claimants on its books to judge whether their benefit income is greater than what officers of the Department estimate they might reasonably expect to earn in work.

The last time the DE conducted this form of investigation was in 1973. At that time officers reported that only 1 per cent of claimants on their books were drawing benefit greater than they might reasonably expect in work although 6 per cent were receiving benefit in the same range as their likely wage from employment. (DE, 1974a, p. 214) A similarly minute proportion was uncovered by the Supplementary Benefits Commission, whose chairman, David Donnison, reported:

> Until July [1975]... we were obliged by the law to seek out all unemployed supplementary benefits claimants who might get more in benefit than they would get in work in order to impose a wage stop which reduced their benefit to a level which did not exceed their wages, after taking account of the expenses they incurred in going to work. We could find so few of them (they amounted to well under 2 per cent of unemployed claimants) that all parties in Parliament agreed to abolish the rule. (Donnison, 1976)

Conclusion

One aspect of the current debate about unemployment is that recent welfare reforms have not only abolished the hardship normally associated with being without work, but they have inevitably led to a large number of people who are voluntarily unemployed. In this chapter we have shown that for an increasing number of people poverty is the inevitable outcome shortly after they have lost their niche in the labour market. We have described how the national insurance system fails to provide for most claimants an income above the official poverty line once they are unemployed. We have also reviewed the evidence on how current levels of benefit have affected claimants' attitudes to work. This shows that, overwhelmingly, unemployed workers wish to regain a foothold in the labour market and that there is no evidence of widespread short-term voluntary unemployment. The reasons for this are partly due to the strength of the work ethic in this country, the individual cost of unemployment (which is the theme of Chapter 6) and the battery of control procedures to prevent abuse. In the next chapter we examine the extent of these measures and their effectiveness.

4 Control measures against abuse

Frank Field

One argument which is put forward to lessen public concern about the current very high level of unemployment compared with other years is that a proportion of this higher unemployment is due to illegal claiming of benefits or to voluntary unemployment. In this chapter we look first at the evidence from official surveys and other research on the attitude of the unemployed to work. We also estimate the extent of benefit wrongly drawn by claimants. The second section looks at the checks the government has imposed to prevent abuse of benefit. Finally, we examine what happened to the 300,000 claimants thrown off benefit between 1968 and 1974 because it was alleged they were workshy. If the argument of the apologists for higher levels of unemployment is correct we would expect to find that these claimants quickly found work once they had been denied benefit. The final section reviews the evidence on this issue.

Official surveys

On a number of occasions the National Assistance Board (NAB) carried out special analyses of unemployed claimants drawing benefit. After completing its first survey the Board reported in 1951: 'In all, out of nearly 60,000 recipients who are classified as "unemployed" at the beginning of December the Board's officers were not prepared to say that more than 7,000 were persons who could be working if they really wanted to work'. (NAB, 1951, p. 8) It is important to stress, however, these surveys covered only a minority of the unemployed – those who were drawing supplementary benefit. It would be wrong, therefore, to conclude that the degree of physical and mental handicap uncovered is typical of all unemployed persons. In the following year the Board reported that these 7,000 claimants average out at 20 or so per office. In 1954, 80,000 unemployed claimants were drawing national assistance and

though these persons were considered fit enough to register at the employment exchange, many of them were physically or mentally handicapped to an extent which made them doubtful candidates for jobs even in conditions of full employment. (NAB, 1954, p. 20)

In 1956 the Board carried out a special enquiry into unemployed claimants drawing assistance, examining the financial and family circumstances of about 32,000 claimants. After completing the survey the Board reported that the

> Results disclosed many problems, but do not support any suggestion that workshyness is extensive, since three out of four of those interviewed, and more than four out of five of those who had been out of work for three or more years were found to be under some sort of physical or mental handicap. (NAB, 1956, p. 43)

The NAB followed up this survey in 1958 by undertaking a special enquiry in Scotland of claimants who were not in full-time work. They took a random sample of men and women under 55 who were out of work and drawing national assistance. The survey showed that of those drawing benefit for nine or more months, over 25 per cent were found on medical examination to be unfit for work or so disabled as to be almost unemployable. A further 60 per cent had some degree of physical or mental ill health or disability likely to have affected their chances of obtaining or keeping employment. More significantly, of the small minority (10 per cent) who the Board's officers thought might be workshy, some 70 per cent proved to be mentally subnormal or unstable. (*ibid.*, pp. 62–3)

This was the final survey carried out by National Assistance Board before it was replaced by the Supplementary Benefits Commission in 1966. The Commission has not carried out any work comparable to the Board's investigations into the attitudes of unemployed claimants. However, the Ministry of Labour (now the Department of Employment) has carried out a number of studies on the unemployed. We now turn to examine their findings to see whether they detected any change in the attitude to work of unemployed claimants.

The Ministry of Labour carried out its first survey in August 1961, when unemployment was 1·4 per cent. The survey found that of 176,000 wholly unemployed men, just over 104,000 or 59 per cent were registered as difficult to place on personal grounds, mostly because of age or physical condition; the latter factor was by no means confined to the registered disabled. Another 10,000, or 6 per cent, were regarded as difficult to place because they had unsatisfactory qualifications. Of the rest, 62,000 or 35 per cent were considered to be good placing propositions, but local opportunities for placing were limited for nearly half of this total. The survey concluded: It is noteworthy that relatively few (eight and a half thousand or 5 per cent) were shown as difficult to place for social reasons (personal record or colour). (Ministry of Labour 1962, p. 131)

The Ministry of Labour carried out a second analysis during October 1964. Unemployment was again low, with only 1·5 per cent of the working population registered as unemployed. After analysing the survey material the Department concluded that:

> The 1964 survey confirms the conclusions reached in 1961 on the chief characteristics of the unemployed .... As in 1961, just over a third of the unemployed men and half of the married women were classified as having good prospects for obtaining work, either in the current situation, or if better opportunities were available .... the remainder were thought likely to have difficulty, in respect of the local employment situation, on account of various personal handicaps. (Ministry of Labour, 1966, p. 156)

The most recent official survey was conducted by the Department of Employment in June 1973. The Department's unemployed register provided a sample of 14,251 men and 2,390 women aged 18 and over. The sample therefore excluded young people, those unemployed who did not register and those who were receiving temporary registrations, or 'People who were expected to get jobs very quickly'. Unemployment stood at 3·9 per cent at the time of the survey.

The survey classified claimants into three groups according to their attitude to work. First, 40 per cent on the adult register in June 1973 were judged to have good or reasonable prospects of finding long-term work, although some of them were limited by the lack of local job opportunities. This is about the same percentage thought in the 1964 survey by local officers to be able to get work without difficulty or who would find difficulty in getting work because of lack of local opportunities. A further 30 per cent of claimants were judged as keen to obtain work but having poor prospects of being successful. The remaining 30 per cent of claimants had poor prospects and were 'somewhat unenthusiastic in their attitude to work'. (DE, 1974, pp. 211–21). The report went on to note 'although in the assessment of local office staff one third of unemployed men are "somewhat unenthusiastic" for work, this does not mean that these men would in practice refuse a job if one was offered to them.' (*ibid.*, p. 212) Indeed, as we will see, these claimants would be in danger of losing benefit if they did. However, tucked away in the report are two important pieces of information which cast some doubt on the meaningfulness of classifying these claimants as 'somewhat unenthusiastic' for work. One of the tables, which is reproduced as Table 4·1, subdivides this total according to whether claimants lived in areas where the DE judged there were good or fair conditions locally for obtaining work. Overwhelmingly those claimants judged to be 'obviously keen' lived in areas where local opportunities were good. The reverse was also true. Those claimants whose attitude to work was 'somewhat unenthusiastic' lived in areas where local officials believed that the prospects of obtaining work were 'poor'. It is possible, therefore, that some men react to the experience of being unemployed, described more fully in the next chapter, adopting a somewhat aggressive attitude to help them face a society which denies them a useful role. Indeed, their attitude reflects a realistic appraisal of the possibility of getting a job.

The second piece of information in the report which casts considerable doubt on the accuracy of moving from the position of 30 per cent of claimants being judged as having an unenthusiastic attitude to work to claiming that this total denotes the increase in voluntary unemployment, is what these claimants were doing six months later. In January 1974 the local officers of the DE were asked to go back to those claimants surveyed in June 1973. Although not all the records were available, the Department concluded that the details on the 88 per cent they were able to investigate were representative.

TABLE 4.1 *Attitude to work*

Prospects of obtaining work	Obviously keen or no reason to doubt that would take suitable job if available	Somewhat unenthusiastic	Total
Men seeking full-time long-term work			
Good or fair, or reasonable but for local conditions	38	2	40
Poor	29	31	60
Total	67	33	100
Women seeking full-time long-term work			
Good or fair, or reasonable but for local conditions	51	3	54
Poor	24 *	22	46
Total	75	25	100
Men and women seeking full-time long-term work			
Good or fair, or reasonable but for local conditions	40	2	42
Poor	28	30	58
Total	68	32	100

(*Source*: DE, 1974a, p. 212)

Two findings on this follow-up survey are relevant to our present discussion. In the first place the Department concluded:

no absolute clear cut judgements can be made about specific groups or even more about particular individuals since over 28 per cent of those considered to have poor prospects had been employed at some time in the following six months, including at least 35 per cent of those who were thought to have poor prospects because of their general attitude to work.

The report also noted

More detailed analyses show that even of those who had been unemployed for over a year at the time of the survey in June 1973, about a fifth had had at least some employment by January 1974. To a certain extent this will have been influenced by the fall in the level of unemployment between June and December 1973. (*ibid.*, p. 215)

Information from official surveys does not, therefore, support the argument of those who claim that recent years have witnessed a change in the attitude to work of a significant number of claimants and that this has inevitably led to a rise in the level of registered unemployed.

The control procedures

Let us suppose for the sake of argument that there has been an increase in the numbers claiming benefit who might, given half a chance, join the ranks of the voluntary unemployed. Would these claimants swell the ranks of the unemployed? To answer this question we examine the whole battery of control procedures operating in the national insurance and supplementary benefits systems to prevent claimants drawing benefit when jobs are available. As we have already noted in our discussions towards the end of Chapter 1, it does appear difficult for considerable numbers of claimants to register their right to unemployment benefit. From the government's own count, we find that at any one time a sixth of unemployed claimants are drawing no benefit whatsoever. Even allowing for those whose claims are in the process of being registered, the number claiming no benefit is probably significant. We say significant because, as we have already noted, although 'about a quarter' of those not claiming benefit on the day of the count 'will in due course be found to have been entitled' the government cannot account for what happens to the remaining three-quarters of non-benefit claims. (*Hansard*, 1975b, col. 215)

We saw in Chapter 3 that unemployed claimants are only eligible for the national insurance unemployment benefit providing they have an adequate insurance record, they are registered for employment at the DE, have not left their last job without good cause and do not refuse employment without a good reason. Failure on any of these counts can lead to the withdrawal of unemployment benefit for up to six weeks and a 40 per cent reduction in a claimant's entitlement to supplementary benefit. These control measures are rigorously enforced. In 1975, 388,000 unemployed persons were disqualified from receiving unemployment benefit for leaving employment voluntarily without just cause, 5,000 for refusing suitable employment without just cause and a further 10,000 for not being available for employment. (*Hansard*, 1976d, col. 544) In addition the government estimate that in December 1975 26,000 had their supplementary benefit reduced for similar reasons. (*Hansard*, 1977e, col. 865)

A further measure of control comes from the DE's squad of officers engaged in tracking down fraudulent claims for unemployment benefit. At the end of June 1976 there were 130 full-time and 174 part-time staff 'who gave the benefit of their special experience and expertise' to this task. In addition 'All of the staff of the benefit service watch for suspicious circumstances which warrant investigation by the specialist staff.' (*Hansard*, 1976h, col. 1133)

The control procedures in the supplementary benefits system aimed at checking voluntary unemployment are even more extensive. The main ones are as follows. In the first place claimants have to register their right to benefit at a local office where they will have to show that they are out of work through no fault of their own, that they have not refused suitable employment without good reason and that their total income for the relevant week is below the specified level of requirements. If the officer in charge of the interview is not satisfied on any of these points, it is normal for no payment to be made until a full investigation into the claimant's circumstances has been completed. This generally includes visiting the claimant's home and collecting information about the claimant from neighbours and local tradespeople. When these enquiries are complete a claimant may still be refused benefit. Local officers have a long checklist in order to help them determine whether claimants should be refused benefit at the outset. The SBC does not keep records of the number of unemployed claimants who are refused benefit under these rules, but the work of welfare rights bodies around the country suggests that the numbers are not inconsiderable.

Since 1961 the DHSS has drawn upon the services of what are known as unemployment review officers. By the end of 1975 their numbers had grown to 107 and their task is to call for interview claimants who, it appears from the records, should or could be in full-time work. During 1975 a squad of officers interviewed 164,533 claimants. As a result of their work 71,328 claimants stopped drawing benefit either before they were called for interview or shortly afterwards. (*Hansard*, 1976j, col. 285) The Department has no information on the circumstances of these claimants once they cease to register for benefit. It may have been that some were working on the side. It is just as likely that as many claimants ceased to draw benefit for fear of being harassed by DHSS officials.

The SBC has a number of other control procedures to check the voluntary unemployment which it regularly uses. In 1951 the first re-establishment centres came into being where unemployed claimants could be sent in order to reintroduce them to the work community. There are now sixteen such centres operating in different parts of the country and over 2,000 claimants in 1975 had their benefit payable on condition that they attended a re-establishment centre. (*Hansard*, 1976g, cols 613–14) The Department has no record of how successful these courses are in helping men back into full-time work.

A further control procedure operates against those claimants who claim to be too ill to undertake full-time work. In 1975 the Commission referred 3,244 claimants for an examination by the Regional Medical Officers of the Health Department. In addition 1,631 unemployed claimants were referred for an examination and an opinion on their capacity for work. (*Hansard*, 1976l, col. 508) Finally, claimants can be and are sued for the non-maintenance of themselves and or their families. The information shows that in 1975 over 600 claimants appeared before the court to defend themselves against this charge.

Like the DE the DHSS employs a squad of special investigators. These are in effect the policemen of the supplementary benefits scheme. The first investigators were appointed in 1954 and their numbers by the beginning of 1975 totalled a little over 380. One of the tasks of these officers is to follow up on claimants suspected of drawing benefit while being in work. In Table 4.2 we present the information on the numbers of investigations carried out and the number of allowances withdrawn or reduced once these investigations had been completed. The number of investigations has grown in recent years and totalled over 15,000 in 1975. A third of these investigations resulted in claimants losing all or part of their benefit.

How much fraud?

How much unemployment and supplementary benefit is wrongly claimed? This is a question which the Fisher Committee considered. The Committee was established by Sir Keith Joseph after the newspapers had run a considerable number of stories on widescale abuse of social security benefit. After surveying all the evidence submitted to it the Committee concluded that £101,961 was wrongly drawn in unemployment benefit in 1971/2 and a little over £1m in supplementary benefit. The supplementary benefit totals included abuse by all groups of supplementary benefit claimants, and both sets of data relate only to detected abuse. (Fisher, 1973, p. 51) We have updated this information in

TABLE 4.2 *Number of investigations and prosecutions of unemployed claimants for undisclosed income*

Type of offence	1972		1973		1974		1975	
	Cases investigated	Allowances withdrawn or reduced	Cases investigated	Allowances withdrawn or reduced	Cases investigated	Allowances withdrawn or reduced	Cases investigated	Allowances withdrawn or reduced
Earnings as employee	7,945	2,901 (37%)	8,696	3,406 (39%)	9,961	3,779 (38%)	11,557	4,441 (38%)
Earnings from self-employment	4,235	1,675 (40%)	4,184	1,629 (39%)	3,945	1,616 (41%)	4,186	1,552 (37%)

(*Source: Hansard*, 1975a, cols 355–6; 1976k, cols 341–2)

TABLE 4.3 *Overpayment and fraud on all social security benefits (1974/5)*

| | Irrecoverable overpayments of benefit recorded during the year | |
	Total	Fraud on the part of the claimant or other person not being a servant of the Department
Family benefits	205,805	32,310
Unemployment benefit	746,292	218,523
Sickness and invalidity benefit	1,754,832	299,243
Maternity benefit	29,840	8,139
Widow's benefit	148,914	65,747
Retirement pension	573,627	24,906
Industrial injury	178,149	20,742
Others	46,280	2,142
Supplementary benefit	5,010,139	1,405,676
Total:	£8,693,878	£2,076,958

(Source: Hansard, 1976e, col. 79)

Table 4.3, from which the following information emerges. Known social security abuse has doubled to a little over £2·2m a year. It is likely that the increase has occurred because of the stepping up of official drives against abuse. We do not know what the true level of social security abuse is but, given the control procedures we have just described, it would be surprising if it was as extensive as some newspaper accounts would have us believe. That it does occur cannot be doubted. The official figures give some idea of the claimants who lose benefit, often finding themselves unrepresented in court, facing charges of fraud. As well as the measure taken by the government to control abuse, we are now aware of an informal policing system which is also at work. This information is given in a study by Dennis Marsden. At the beginning of his study, Marsden makes it quite clear that his small sample of unemployed persons is not representative of all the unemployed. But the advantage of his approach was that he managed to gain their confidence and talk to them about the experience of being workless in a way that few other investigators have managed. In doing so, claimants told him not only why they worked on the side but the strict unofficial policing system which operates to make sure that no one claimant draws an unfair proportion of these perks.

From what men said, fiddling filled a number of needs. It brought them once again the sense of control over their lives which some of them had clearly valued in work. It brought money that was their own and not the state's or their wives'. It brought freedom to spend once again, because the extra money from fiddling insulated the men's drinking and social needs from the family budget. (Marsden and Duff, 1975, p. 246)

Elsewhere in the study Marsden reports that a number of men first began to take a job on the side when they found they were unable to look after the basic needs of their families from their dole payments. Working on the side therefore provided money to buy the children shoes or to help pay the fuel bills. But the study also reported:

Both in the work and the freedom to spend, fiddling brought male companionship. Workless men's drinking was seen as a form of abuse – paradoxically drinking is regarded by the public as indicating at one and the same time that benefits are too high *and* that men are leaving their families short of money. But on the evidence of study, less skilled, workless men went out drinking partly because of pressures in the home. Out of work they were strongly drawn to the masculine world of the street corner, the club and the pub. And also they needed to maintain social relationships with the work group to keep in the running for jobs. (*ibid.*, p. 246–7)

In addition 'fiddling kept alive an individual's self-respect in the face of evidence that employers did not want him. Fiddling was a protection against the charge that he was "doing nothing".' (*ibid.*, p. 249) A job on the side protected the workless against this charge as well as keeping them active and in shape for work. But before anyone concludes from this evidence that abuse of benefit must be widescale, they also need to consider another finding from Marsden's research. This study showed that it was almost as if Adam Smith's 'hidden hand' operated at a local level to ensure that no one person gained too great a reward from a job on the side. 'In fact, from what the workless said, fiddling was closely policed informally by local opinion and by anonymous letters from neighbours if a fiddler was thought to be getting more than his fair share of additional income.' (*ibid.*, p. 247) The more an unemployed claimant fiddled the less there would be available for other claimants. Likewise, as unemployment rose so there were more workless competing in the unofficial labour market. 'So it might be suggested that, paradoxically, in times of high unemployment the less vigilant the authorities, the more tightly will market forces operate to keep down fiddlers' gain from irregular work.' (*ibid.*, p. 247)

Evidence from official surveys on the attitude to work of unemployed claimants, together with details on the extensive control procedures to prevent abuse, should be sufficient in undermining the arguments of those who claim we have witnessed in recent years a significant increase in the numbers of people who prefer not to work for the going market rate but to draw benefit. But still the argument persists and so we therefore conclude this chapter with a case study of what became known as the four-week rule. The rule was introduced in the middle of 1968 because it was believed that a considerable number of claimants preferred to remain idle than to set about seeking suitable employment. The DHSS obviously believed that those claimants who most needed to have their minds concentrated on finding work were unskilled, physically fit men under the age of 45 who were living in areas where it was 'thought' suitable job opportunities existed. These claimants were told, on claiming supplementary benefit, that their entitlement would be withdrawn after four weeks as they should be able to find work during this period – hence the name, the four-week rule. Married men, skilled workers and women were allowed three months before the rule was applied, while men between 45 and 60 and those not fully fit were given up to six months to find work before their supplementary benefit was curtailed. Men over 60 were allowed a year's grace.

How did this rule work out in practice? The argument of critics has been that because social security benefits are generous, considerable numbers of people prefer voluntary unemployment to work, particularly for short periods during the year. As the four-week rule resulted in the mass withdrawal of benefit from those claimants against whom the charge of voluntary unemployment is made, we can put these criticisms under the microscope. When people are reduced to destitution, do they take jobs or do they remain unemployed because there are no jobs available? In order to answer these questions we draw on the only major published piece of research into the effects of the four-week rule. (Meacher, 1974) The survey was of 7,074 men in the North, Midlands, South East and South West of the country who were contacted in 1973. Of these it was found that 98 claimants had had the four-week rule applied against them.

Molly Meacher wrote up the findings of the research during 1973. From the introduction of the rule in 1968 to that point in time over 275,000 men all over Britain had been penalised under the rule. If we suppose that the claimants in the survey were representative of other claimants against whom the four-week rule had been applied, what is the national picture which emerges? Grossing up the survey figures, Molly Meacher concluded that during the period from October 1968 to March 1973 (and it is important that the rule operated for almost a full year after this date until it was suspended during the three-day week) about 137,000 men were deprived of benefit after four weeks despite remaining unemployed at the time. Withdrawal of benefit did not ensure that these claimants found a niche in the labour market. When one looks at the groups making up this total, this is not surprising. For instance, even though 88,000 'probably had no income whatsoever when their benefit was withdrawn' and a further 49,000 claimants had 'probably only had a small amount of unemployment benefit each week, but insufficient to live on and in many cases not even enough to pay the rent', the survey showed that 55,000 mentally and physically ill claimants had the four-week rule applied against them. (*ibid*., p. 104–5)

The rule was intended to force people into jobs. But with none available, other means of livelihood had to be sought. The survey showed that not an inconsiderable number of men were driven back by the four-week rule to the one 'solution' which was open to them, namely, thieving. Grossing the figure up to the national level, Molly Meacher estimated that 25,000 turned to crime after being denied benefit. More important, something like 27,000 thousand men 'resorted to crime for the first time in their lives during the weeks following withdrawal of benefit.' (*ibid*., p. 104). Others who were unable to find work moved in and lived off their girlfriends, while others took to male prostitution. Hardly the results expected by those who thought the four-week rule would reinforce the Protestant work ethic.

Conclusion

One argument currently deployed in public debate which aims at quelling anxiety about the very significant increase in the level of unemployment during the last few years is that there has been a significant increase in the numbers of voluntarily unemployed. The most sophisticated of debaters argue not for a 'tightening up' against these claimants but a better public understanding of the higher level of unemployment. In this chapter we have tried to examine the evidence available which underpins this argument. We have examined all the official surveys on unemployed claimants which show that there has not been a significant change in claimants' attitudes to work during a period when critics point to the introduction of welfare reforms aimed at improving the relative income of claimants. But even if there had been an increase in claimants wishing to be voluntarily unemployed, both the DE and the DHSS have a whole battery of control procedures aimed at preventing the abuse of social benefits. Moreover, we have lived through a period during which the DHSS operated the four-week rule. There could be no better test of the 'voluntary unemployed' thesis than the operation of this rule. It was found that even when claimants had their minds concentrated on finding a job because they had lost what was often their only source of income, large numbers were unable to find work. This is not surprising as unemployment, measured by the official statistics, was rising for practically the whole period during which the rule was in operation. A rather inconvenient finding for those who are mainly concerned to explain away the unemployed when their numbers are rising.

5 Poverty and unemployment in Liverpool

Clare Dennehy and Jill Sullivan

Introduction

The material collected for this chapter attempts to highlight the problems being faced at the present time by a number of the unemployed. We specifically selected a part of Liverpool 8 for our study because it is our aim to present a picture of unemployment in one of Britain's blackspots. Liverpool and the North-West have a higher-than-average rate of unemployment and, likewise, Liverpool 8 has been harder hit than the rest of Liverpool. Thus it will be understood that our small study of one tiny area in Britain is not intended to illustrate the unemployment situation of the whole of the United Kingdom in the late 70s but is rather a snapshot of two streets selected at random, surveyed in a particular week at the end of 1976. Nevertheless, we hope it will be a useful illustration of the many difficulties facing those workers who find that they are no longer allowed to contribute as members of the nation's work force.

The survey

Having chosen two neighbouring streets in Liverpool 8 and armed with a brief initial questionnaire, we first set out to ascertain general information about the number of people in each household, their ages, and their employment status, i.e. whether they were retired, working full-time, working part-time or unemployed. The unemployed were asked whether they received benefits, were registered at the Employment Exchange, the length of their unemployment and finally, from what source they were most hopeful of finding a job. Those currently in work were asked if they had been unemployed for any period during the past couple of years. The information collected allowed us to gain a general impression of the true level of unemployment in the two streets. We were also able to see what use the unemployed made of registering for benefit and of the employment services in finding jobs. Furthermore, we gained some idea of how effective the social security system is in protecting the living standards of people interviewed. After the initial survey of the two streets we returned to seven households, first, where there was somebody unemployed and second, where there were now people in work who had been previously unemployed, in order to get a more vivid and detailed picture of life on the dole in Liverpool 8 in 1976, how particular families managed their finances, whether they found themselves worse or better off in or out of work, what hopes they had of finding a job and by what means. The information gained from this second, more detailed, questionnaire is presented in the form of seven case studies as the second half of this chapter.

The level of unemployment in one of Britain's blackspots

The two streets covered by the survey were similar in appearance, both containing terraced houses, built in 1875, most of which were privately rented and a few privately owned. In the first street we surveyed there were forty-six occupied houses (originally the street probably had about sixty houses). From these we obtained twenty-seven responses, eleven 'no replies' after calling at least three times, and eight people refused to co-operate with the survey, giving a response rate of 58·7 per cent. The second street we surveyed was considerably more dilapidated. Of the forty houses still standing, we got a response from twenty-two, thirteen 'no replies' after calling at least three times and five refusals – a response rate of 55 per cent. Thus our total survey response rate was 57 per cent. In the twenty-seven houses in the first street we found that there were sixty-six adults, thirty-two of whom were working and thirty-four not working, and in the second street we found fifty-two adults, twenty-seven of whom were in work and twenty-five not working. There were twenty-seven children in the first street and thirty-four in the second.

In Table 5.1 we detail the occupational status of those adults of both streets who were not in work. From this we can see variations in the populations of the two streets. For example, in the second street housewives formed a much larger proportion of the non-working adult population. There were eleven, forming 44 per cent, whereas in the first street there were only eight housewives, forming only 23·5 per cent of the non-working population. However Street No. 2 contained a larger proportion of children and this would account for the higher percentage of married women not working. We can also see that in the first street people of retirement age formed about 15 per cent of the total adults interviewed in that street, whilst in the second street they formed 11·5 per cent.

We can now calculate the true level of unemployment in the two streets. Of the sixty-six adults in Street No. 1, ten were retired, leaving a total of fifty-six of working age. We found eleven were unemployed, which gives

TABLE 5.1 *Employment status of those not working*

	Street No. 1	Street No. 2
Pensioners	10	6
Housewives	8	11
Students	5	0
Unemployed	11	7
In prison	0	1
Total	34	25

us an unemployment rate of almost 20 per cent. In the second street six of the fifty-two adults were above working age. Of the remaining forty-six, seven were unemployed, giving us an unemployment rate of just over 15 per cent. We can say therefore that the unemployment rate in the part of Liverpool covered by our survey at the end of 1976 was 17·4 per cent – of the hundred and two adults eligible for work, eighteen were unemployed. However, it is possible that a number of the women classified as housewives who were not registered at the Exchange and who had grown-up children would have been actively seeking work had the general employment situation been more hopeful.

We now turn to look at the unemployed themselves. In Table 5.2 we have divided them according to marital status, subdividing single people between those who had just left school and those who had been in work previously but had lost their jobs. We have also classified them according to length of time of unemployment. It is interesting to note that the two school leavers unemployed were female, perhaps accounted for by the fact that job creation schemes in the area, although few and far between, are mainly for the benefit of boys leaving school. During our survey of the two streets we came across two or three boys of school leaving age who had been fortunate enough to benefit from such a scheme, either in landscaping or in the furniture making project. There appeared to be nothing comparable for girls. The two females, one aged 18 and the other 19, under the classification 'single people' had been in employment since leaving school but were now unable to get back into the labour market. The other two females, one with a young baby and the other with no children had been unemployed for four to six months. However, in all but one classification male unemployment predominates.

Three males had been out of work for less than three months, two between four and six months, two between a year and eighteen months and five had been out of work for more than two years. Of these five, four were married, two with children.

TABLE 5.2 *Marital status, sex and length of time unemployed*

	School leavers		Single people (excluding school leavers)		Married (without children)		Married (with children)		Total	
	M	F	M	F	M	F	M	F	M	F
Up to 3 mths			1		2*				3	
4–6 mths		1	1			1		1	1	3
7–12 mths		1		2			1		1	3
13–18 mths			1				1		2	
19–24 mths										
Over 24 mths			1		2**		2		5	
Total									12	6

* One not registered at Exchange – in between jobs.
** One registered as sick in December 1976.

The employment services

Two aspects of the current unemployment situation for unskilled workers in Liverpool 8 were highlighted both by the tenants of the two streets surveyed and by a visit to the local Job Centre. The first relates to jobs available for school leavers. The impression gained from a number of interviewees was that most of the jobs for the under-18s paid around £13 and those relating to 'men's work' consisted largely of unskilled jobs paying £30 a week; most interviewees added that after deductions and travelling expenses they would be worse off in employment than on benefit. A visit to the Job Centre confirmed the scarcity of employment opportunities available to all groups of workers, both skilled and non-skilled, young and old. Most of the boards had a number of gaps and large spaces between cards.

For school leavers there were just a handful of jobs available. The few labouring vacancies open to them offered rates of between £13 and £16 and most specified that applicants had to have been unemployed for six months. Employers in this instance were obviously taking advantage of the government's scheme whereby the firm is paid a subsidy of £10 a week for six months for employing someone who had not been in work for the last twenty-six weeks. Cards advertising shop jobs were also hard to find, and these offered £17.70 at 17 and £18 at 18. Office jobs were slightly more in evidence and rates ranged from £12, for a junior shorthand typist aged 17–18, to £18. Practically all the office vacancies required applicants to have GCE O level English and in some cases they required Maths as well. For the 18-plus age group the jobs advertised on the day in question were mainly skilled occupations or jobs requiring previous experience. Rates ranged from £40 to £73 for qualified electricians, £36.80 to £52 for driving jobs, £36 to £60 for cutters, fitters, etc. Full-time office jobs for women ranged from £20 to £44; part-time vacancies mainly for domestic work or cleaning paid about £6.50.

A large proportion of jobs advertised were outside the Liverpool area, especially in the hotel and catering sector. So too were a large proportion of jobs in manufacturing industries. However most of the jobs for school leavers, in shops and offices, were located in Liverpool or the surrounding area. Another point, indicative of the current employment scene, was the fact that some of the jobs mentioned above were for 'temporary' staff, thus illustrating the uncertainty of long-term employment in some trades. The Job Centre itself told us that for every one vacancy there are thirty-five unemployed registrants.

One of the points to emerge strongly from our investigations of the two streets was how ineffective both the Job Centre and the Employment Exchange appeared to be in helping the unemployed find jobs. Of course there is relatively little they can do, given the drastic fall in the number of jobs available. But it is interesting to note that of those who had recently suffered unemployment and were now in work none told us that they had found either the Job Centre or the Exchange or any other official body helpful in finding them a job. This was true for both school leavers and older workers. One school leaver told us of her experiences – she had hardly ever been offered a job by the Exchange and when they did arrange an interview, they sent twenty people after the same job. She had also been told that if she wanted a job she would have to get to the Exchange as early as 8 a.m. although they did not open until 9 a.m. Another school leaver had been unemployed for three months before finding a job, as a shop assistant, through a newspaper. The Job Centre had not come up with one job during that time.

Neither did older people find the Centre or the Exchange helpful. One man told us he had found his job as an electrician with the Corporation by filling in a form at the Corporation and nine months later they offered him a job. Meanwhile he had pursued twenty or thirty on his own. He did not feel the Exchange was helpful: 'if you're skilled, its a drawback, you get offered jobs for kids'. Similarly, another man, this time unskilled, concentrated entirely (after a few months of attending the Exchange) on the Corporation and was eventually successful in obtaining work as a roadsweeper. Two other men had been unemployed in the last two years, and had both decided after fruitless searching for a job to become self-employed, one as a taxi-driver and the other as a mechanic.

As our visit to the Job Centre confirmed, many of the jobs were outside the Liverpool area and many claimants considered these to be extremely unreliable. Two or three people said they were often temporary. Also there was very little hard information offered by the Centre on these, i.e. rates of pay, etc. Furthermore, from the evidence gathered in the questionnaire, it appeared that none of those interviewed were aware that help, in the form of travelling or removal expenses, was available to those willing to seek work outside Liverpool. Most of the people we spoke to told us that they could not afford the financial risk of chasing jobs outside of Liverpool, and that the rates of pay offered would not compensate for the amount paid in fares if they were to be successful in finding employment outside the city.

Government training schemes also came in for a lot of criticism from residents; for example, we detail in our study of Mr Daniels his unfortunate experience when training as a plasterer. When after three months' work he found himself back on the dole he came to the conclusion that the money would have been better spent on providing nurseries so that women could get part-time work. Another man told us that it was not worth going on a retraining scheme because 'they only pay your expenses and you can't get a job afterwards anyway'. Yet another felt that government retraining schemes were positively harmful in that they created more problems by training men and women for trades, so adding even further to the number of people chasing after skilled jobs. By offering unskilled men the chance to better themselves by training for a trade, the government was only shifting the bulk of the unemployed in manufacturing industry from the unskilled sector to the skilled. Many people felt that since jobs in manufacturing industry were so scarce as to be practically non-existent, or else poorly paid and very insecure, so many being temporary, it would be a much better bet to stick to finding something locally, which inevitably meant something with the local council.

We have noted earlier that no one told us that they had found a job through either the Job Centre or Employment Exchange. On the whole people seemed to be much more confident of finding a job by their own efforts, either by hearing of one on the off chance, perhaps through friends or in a pub, or by persistent applications to the local council. Most looked in papers, but, although one school leaver had been lucky there, the general feeling was that jobs advertised were usually taken by the time one got to a phone. We were also told by one man that unskilled jobs were hardly ever advertised in the papers – employers just went down to the nearest street corner to find men.

Living standards of those working and the unemployed

We have seen in the previous section that the vast majority of jobs available to the residents of the area of our survey paid very badly, particularly labouring jobs, in many cases affording a man no more than what he would get from social security. This is particularly true in the case of school leavers, and married men with children to support. This fact is of considerable relevance to the current debate about workers being better off on social security. However, the evidence from our study of this area of Liverpool would suggest that contrary to popular belief, it is low wages rather than high unemployment benefits that is the principal cause of this myth. Moreover, we found that some of those dependent on these benefits, far from living a life of luxury, were not in receipt of their full entitlement and consequently suffered a lower standard of living than they need have done.

Throughout the period of our survey we were made increasingly aware of the bitterness of some of those currently working for such low wages towards their unemployed neighbours who they thought (often wrongly) enjoyed a higher standard of living. Furthermore, we became conscious of a similar feeling of bitterness amongst some of the unemployed men we met, particularly those with large families, who saw their chances of ever finding a job that would pay them enough to support their children as practically non-existent. These men resented their enforced idleness and some felt themselves to be 'scroungers' through no fault of their own. One family especially comes to mind: we were told by the wife of a man who had been out of work for two years and had several children that her husband did not wish to talk of his experiences of unemployment – he had come increasingly to think of himself as a 'scrounger' relieving the state of vast sums of money each week to support his large family, but seeing no way out of this situation. Our visit to the Job Centre confirmed his assessment of the hopeless situation; there was not one job advertised which would remotely have paid him a net wage equal to his benefit. A further example of the pressure on the unemployed with large families is the case that we were told about on several occasions of a father with four children, who had become so desperate about being unemployed and consequent labelling as a 'scrounger' that he had committed suicide.

Nevertheless, although the above two examples are horrifying, one also sympathises with other men with children who are working for low wages. One man who was in work after a spell of twelve months' unemployment found himself obliged to do overtime (sometimes working a $6^{1}/_{2}$-day week) in order to maintain the standard of living he had had out of work and 'to get extras for the kids'. He was of the opinion that 'the present system only encourages people to stay on the dole' and 'in this country you are definitely penalised for having children'.

This man also made another very important point, on which much of the discussion about the relative living standards of the low-paid workers and the unemployed man is relevant. If, as he is forced to do, you have to work for a subsistence wage, in reality you are scarcely less dependent on state support than are the unemployed, as you become one of that group of workers who are eligible for some kind of income support, in the form of family income supplement, free school meals, rent and rate rebates, welfare foods, etc. And when so many people in a community are forced either by their low wages or lack of a job to depend on welfare benefits to lift them to the state's poverty line income, then readily available information about them, who is entitled to what and how it can be obtained, is absolutely crucial. Unfortunately, during the course of our survey, we found that an important cause of the hardship and poverty that both the unemployed and those in work suffered was the universal ignorance about welfare benefits, not only among the residents but also among those in the official sector.

The families reported that the officers of the local DHSS office at no time ever volunteered information on extra benefits, for example extra help for heating, without first being asked, and even then there were several instances where people were misinformed. But the effect of this sort of lack of information about entitlement to benefits is even more devastating for those totally dependent on the welfare, i.e. the unemployed. One unemployed man had not realised that it was possible to claim supplementary benefit in spite of having savings, which he consequently used up. He is now in work and receives 60p family income supplement, which should provide him with a passport to other welfare benefits. However, his wife, on being asked whether the children got free school meals, told us that 'they work it out differently here, they take into account what you earn, family allowances, rent and work it out on what is left.' Consequently they unnecessarily spent £3.25 a week on school meals. His wife was also worried about the welfare milk they did get because 'we have been claiming milk from the welfare but that's running out soon and I don't know whether we will be able to claim after his extra £2.50.'

It became increasingly apparent to us that unless people were prepared to plough through official literature, not always on show, they were unlikely to get any assistance from officials. The man mentioned above had used up his savings because he did not have access to 'the right forms'. Likewise, it should be noted that no one receiving unemployment benefit or supplementary benefit ever knew how it had been calculated. We were told it was customary practice to have to wait for the full amount due, usually five weeks. Several people were unable to tell us whether their money was made up of earnings-related supplement, flat-rate unemployment benefit or supplementary benefit, or if they received extra weekly additions. It should be noted that the one person who could say definitely that they received an exceptional circumstances allowance (for a special diet) was a pensioner. Given the appalling condition of the houses we saw, one would have thought that many families should have been receiving assistance with their heating bills. In fact, we came across many who did not use one or more rooms because of the damp. However, nobody told us they received an extra weekly addition. One couple who had a baby with pneumonia were aware that they should get one, but did not know whether it was included in their weekly allowance. In fact when we worked out their benefit we discovered that they were receiving a heating allowance of 35p a week, the lowest amount available. In view of their baby's health and the damp condition of their house it seemed to us that they should have been getting a higher rate.

Similarly, although we came across five men who had been unemployed for over two years, none of them told us that they had been successful in getting an exceptional needs payment for replacement of clothes, furniture, etc. The only exceptional needs payment we had evidence of was one for £15 given two years ago to a family to buy four pairs of shoes. All the other families we spoke to had either not applied for extra help because they were unaware it might be available, or because the attitude of officials humiliated them, or had applied and had been refused. One single man enquiring about extra help for pots and pans had been told that 'they only get so much money from the government and it's got to last the whole year for everyone'.

Because of the confusion surrounding entitlement to benefit and the low rates of pay offered in the area surveyed, it is difficult to make any sort of meaningful statement about the relative living standards of those in work as opposed to those of the unemployed. However, financial aspects apart, those in work did have other advantages. They do not have to face each day wondering whether an employment opportunity will be forthcoming and feeling of hopelessness when it is not. They do not have to force themselves to chase jobs knowing that another thirty or so people would also be after the same vacancy. Neither do they have to wonder how they will pass the long hours of the day with no money to help alleviate the boredom, nor stand up to the final humiliation of 'living off the state' with all the stigma the phrase implies.

We now turn to the interviews with some of the families living in the two streets to detail the first-hand experience of life in a poor area when unemployment is at a postwar record.

Young unemployed

June Palmer lives with her parents, two sisters and her grandfather, Mr Howard. She has been in and out of work since leaving school two-and-a-half years ago. She worked at Whites, a department store, as a sales assistant and this job lasted for nine months. Since then she has been largely out of work, although the odd job as a sales assistant, or working in a hotel in Wales, shows that she still wants to work and does take up an opportunity even if it is some distance away.

June, like a number of other people we spoke to, has a very confused view of her social security rights. She now draws £12·90 a week but is unclear whether this is unemployment or supplementary benefit. She read in the press of increases in benefits to take place in the middle of November although she did not receive her increase until a week later. When she raised this at the local office she was told that 'nothing could be done about it'. June also has no idea whether she has at any time drawn earnings-related benefit. The family's dealings with social security have never been happy or, according to them, satisfactory. When she first registered for benefit she was paid £5·05 each week for eight weeks. The office claimed that June had left her job without good cause. With the support of her mother, June protested against this decision and asked to go to a tribunal. She was then given a giro cheque for £48. As June's grandfather said, 'You wouldn't be given that, would you, if they weren't trying to hide something.'

Mr Howard's attitude to social security is currently affected by a recent brush with a local officer. The latter had come round during the day to check up on June, and the family presumed that this was to see whether she was working on the side. He asked Mr Howard 'Are you having a day off?' Mr Howard replied that he had been retired since last January. He had worked until he was 69 and considered the officer's question as 'damn cheek'.

June still makes considerable efforts to find work. She goes to the local Employment Exchange about four times a week, partly because she wants a job, but also because the local staff have 'threatened her'. They told her that they will 'stop the dole' unless she goes down to the local office. Each trip costs June 24p in fares. The letter which told her to report daily to the Exchange was taken away on one of her trips to the Exchange. No pressure has been put on June to find work outside the area but one of the first questions she was asked was whether she would be prepared to join the RAF. She was not enthusiastic about this idea. Other jobs have been offered by the Exchange, the last one as a shop assistant at £13 a week. June explained that if she had accepted this job she would have been getting less money than she does on benefit, after taking into account fares and other expenses of going to work. June thinks that a reasonable salary for her would be £20 a week. However from the evidence gathered at the local Job Centre, and from the comments of other people in the area, £13 seems about the average on offer to school leavers and the under-18s. The family added that from their experience they thought that as soon as young workers reached the age of 18 they were sacked and their jobs offered to younger workers, thus keeping the wages bill as low as possible.

June estimates that she has gone after about fifty jobs, most from newspaper advertisements. She has never had a reply to any of these applications. The family said that it is difficult to get a job if you live in Liverpool 8 as the area has a bad name. An illustration of how tight the job market is was given by Mr Howard, who said that firms often put small adverts in the local paper thanking applicants who had applied for jobs and saying that they could not possibly write to thank each individual enquirer. Mrs Palmer verified this by adding that when she went for an interview for her present job as a part-time canteen assistant there were twenty applicants within the space of a quarter of an hour. Apart from looking for jobs in the local paper, June also relies on friends and relatives for information about possible vacancies. She reckons that most of her near misses have been jobs suggested by friends.

June gets very bored at home all day, although she helps her mother with the chores. She contributes to the family budget and has very little money left for clothes and the other things that most 18-year-olds like to be able to buy. The Palmers live in a three-bedroomed house, one of which is not used because of continual damp from broken tiles, and this makes sleeping arrangements extremely difficult, even for the most friendly of families. June is hoping to get married sometime this year and this will help to alleviate the housing situation for the family somewhat. However although June's fiancé is working she is unable to save anything towards the cost of getting married and setting up a new home. She hopes that after her 18th birthday she will be able to get a job in either a bingo hall or club and that eventually things will be much easier for her.

Unemployed and unskilled

Mr Green, a married man with two very young children, has been out of work since June 1975. Although Mr and Mrs Green are very dispirited about their situation, having only been married a short while before Mr Green became unemployed, they are still vaguely hopeful about their future. 'You have to look on the bright side, don't you – something will turn up.'

Mr Green was employed for five years as a floor layer, before which he was in the merchant navy. He became redundant when the firm he worked for went bankrupt. Although there were promises of redundancy pay no money has ever materialised. In the last year of employment he earned between £20 and £36 net a week, working on average nine to ten hours a day. He was paid a basic wage plus a supplement calculated on the amount of yardage laid.

During the first six months of unemployment Mr Green received flat-rate unemployment benefit plus earnings-related supplement, totalling £22·50. The family, which at this time comprised Mr and Mrs Green and one child, then had to exist on flat-rate unemployment benefit of £20·50 for another six months before receiving supplementary benefit of £23 a week. This sum has now been increased to £30 a week, to cover the cost of feeding, clothing and housing Mr and Mrs Green and two small children. No delays were experienced in receiving benefit but the Greens have never been informed of any of their rights or told how their benefit has been worked out. They have asked the local office for money to buy wardrobes but this request was turned down.

To be able to live adequately Mr Green estimates that he would need to find a job giving him at least £40 a week net and ideally £50. However, from his experiences over the last months he is not hopeful on this score. He is registered at the Employment Exchange but says he has not found them very helpful. Apart from the time when he received a telegram informing him of a vacancy and arrived for an interview only to be told that the job had gone two weeks earlier, the Employment Exchange have been unable to find him any other jobs. He goes to the Job Centre from time to time but says that most of the advertisements are 'just for kids – they pay such low wages we couldn't possibly live on them – it is difficult enough to manage on £30 a week now'. Mr Green is also prepared to take a labouring job and uses the newspaper as another source of possible employment opportunities. Friends and relatives also keep their eyes open for him and Mr Green does the rounds of building sites but is always told that there is nothing going. Not one job has been offered to him during his time of unemployment. No pressure has been put on him to find work outside the area but he would be prepared to do this even though most of the Green family live in Liverpool, if he knew how to go about it. He was not aware that it was possible to receive payment of expenses while looking for work in other towns or that he could receive help with removal expenses. However, if the Greens did take this course of action they would have to overcome the problem of selling their house, for which they paid £250, before being able to settle anywhere else. Mr Green is also not very hopeful about the help afforded by attending a Government Retraining Centre. 'They only pay your expenses and you can't get jobs afterwards'.

The effect of unemployment on the Greens has been one of demoralisation. From the start of their married life they have had to struggle desperately to make ends meet. They have not had an evening out together since they married except for the one time when friends paid for them to go to a dance. Mr Green goes to the pub on a Saturday night but he is only able to do this because friends buy him a drink. He spends the rest of his time reading the paper, watching the television or looking for a job. They never have any money to buy extras for their children, and have barely enough for the basic necessities. Their eldest child, aged 15 months, is in need of a new winter coat but the Greens cannot afford one. Mrs Green won't buy from clothing clubs and is reluctant to go to jumble sales as she feels that this would be the final degradation. The lack of variety in their food reinforces the monotony of their life. They very rarely eat meat and buy mostly tinned as opposed to fresh food because it is cheaper. Mrs Green estimates that she spends about £15 a week on food, and toiletries, but cannot afford to buy the baby, aged 6 weeks, the proper milk, and so has to give her evaporated milk and rusks. They never have a cooked breakfast as they can't afford one.

Their house, which is terraced and built around 1875, is in a very bad condition. It is damp all the way through, has no bathroom or hot water. They have no money to decorate or repair it, and can only heat two rooms, the living room and the baby's bedroom. Their fuel bills total about £4·80 a week, other expenses, including laundry, TV rental, insurance, HP and newspapers total £5·04. They bought their house, borrowing the £250 purchase price from Mrs Green's father, and repay this loan at £5 a week. But they do not get any help from the social security with this payment as they would if they were renting a house. (However, had they a proper mortgage, they would be given help to cover the interest charges.) On top of this they pay £1·93 a week rates. They are hoping that when the street is demolished they will recoup the £250 from the Council.

Mrs Green is able to budget right down to the last penny and the family have no arrears hanging over them. They do not have any money put by for emergencies and the very little amount of furniture in the house has been given to them. They have received no help whatsoever from social security for buying clothes or household goods and only receive visits 'to see if conditions are still the same'. Their one hope at the moment for a better future is the time when the baby is older and Mrs Green can go out to work. That is, of course, assuming that she will be able to find suitable employment.

Past experiences

Living across the road from the Greens are another young married couple, Mr and Mrs Marsden, who have three small children. At the moment the Marsdens enjoy somewhat more security than the Greens because Mr Marsden is employed as an electrician with the Corporation and has been in this employment for the last eighteen months. However, he has had a number of spells of unemployment. The most recent period lasted from December 1973 to June 1975. During this time he received unemployment benefit of £22.40 but doesn't know whether this included earnings-related benefit. He received benefit as soon as he became unemployed but had to wait four to five weeks before receiving the correct rate. This, Mr Marsden added, 'happens to everybody in the area'. When asked whether it had been explained to him just how his benefit had been worked out he replied 'No, you're never aware of any of your rights.' After one year unemployment benefit stopped and Mr Marsden received supplementary benefit instead. He says that he got less on supplementary benefit and remembers that he received about £20.

During his eighteen-month spell of unemployment Mr Marsden recalls that he was offered three jobs. They were all out of town, i.e. in Crosby and Southport, and paid about £40 a week. He explained that it would have been impossible for him to take any of them because he would not have been able to afford the expenses of travelling or of taking digs. At the time he was not aware of any scheme that would help in meeting removal expenses if he left Liverpool to work in another town, or of the fact that he could claim expenses when looking for work in other areas.

Mr Marsden estimates that he went after between thirty and forty jobs during this time, mostly found by himself via newspapers or through friends. He always found the same situation – too many applicants chasing one job. He added that he realised the situation is much worse now than it was then. He felt that the Government Retraining Scheme had helped to create more problems by training men and women for trades, so adding even further to the number of applicants chasing after one job. For the first six months of his unemployment he used to visit the Job Centre once or twice a week but became disheartened at his lack of success in finding a job. He then left his telephone number with the Centre and asked them to ring him if anything suitable came in. He found this period of unemployment very worrying financially and depressing because of his lack of success. He used to fill in his time by going to jumble sales, picking up old pieces of furniture very cheaply, and renovating them for use in his home. Most of their furniture had been acquired this way.

The Marsdens never received any extra money from social security to cover the cost of much-needed clothes for the children or household goods. They were very strong in their denouncement of the officials at their local DHSS office whom they felt to be extremely officious and lacking in any understanding of their situation. 'It's degrading enough to have to go on benefit – it's even more degrading to go to our local office, they treat you very badly.' Happily Mr Marsden eventually got a job with the Corporation, but this was through his own efforts. He earns £40 gross for a 45-hour week, but added that when he is on bonus work he can earn £50 to £60 a week. However, he added that bonus work was very hard work and said 'You shouldn't have to work like that for a decent wage.' The Marsdens thought that a decent wage was about £80 a week gross for a skilled worker.

Although the Marsdens feel that they are financially better off now than they were when Mr Marsden was unemployed, they still have to budget very carefully to make ends meet. They run a car, but this is mainly used by Mr Marsden to travel the sixteen miles to and from work. They have one night out a week at the local legion club. They usually manage to have a holiday once a year but only because they stay rent free in a friend's caravan. Christmas, however, is a special problem. It is the only time the three children get any new clothes, this year it was a jumper each. All their other clothes come from jumble sales.

Mrs Marsden estimated that she spends £20 to £25 on food, including £3 on soap powders, etc. She doesn't buy joints of meat any more and has cut down on cheese, bacon, cooked meats, etc. Gas and electricity amount to approximately £25 a quarter. £6 a week goes on petrol and Mr Marsden has to put aside about £150 during the year to tax, insure and maintain the car. They pay £3·31 fortnightly for insurance and, before buying a washing machine recently, Mrs Marsden said she spent about £7 a week in the launderette. (She explained that this was because two of their children were bedwetters.) The purchase of the washing machine will, in the long run, save them money. She is able to give all the children a cooked breakfast and they have a good midday meal at school which costs £2·25 a week (although they might well be eligible for free school meals). The house, for which they pay £3·25 a week rent and rates, looks much the same as the rest of the street from the outside. Inside it is quite modestly, though comfortably, furnished and at first sight there are no glaring defects. However, Mr Marsden pointed out that the step from the living room down into the kitchen should not be there. It is where the back of the house has subsided and sunk into the ground about a foot. He thinks there is a real danger of the whole of the back of the house coming away from the rest. It is something they have had to live with for a long time and will have to endure for some years ahead.

Even though Mr Marsden is now working they have not been able to save any money for emergencies. They hope to remedy this when Mrs Marsden starts looking for work in 1977. She is a trained nurse and is hoping to get a part-time job to help supplement her husband's income.

Unemployed housewife

Mrs Browning is a young housewife, currently looking for an office job, but without much success. She is a trained telephonist but is prepared to do any sort of clerical work. She has never before had a period of unemployment and only left her last job in December 1975 to have a baby. Mr Browning is in full-time employment and works as a manager at a local bakery. Although they are able to manage on his wage, they miss the money that Mrs Browning was able to add to their income. In her previous employment she earned £18 for a 40-hour week. She took home £15 out of which she had to pay £2·40 fares. Although Mrs Browning admits that this was not a good wage, it was better than the amount of benefit she receives. She received a maternity allowance of £11·10 until two weeks after her baby was born and then received unemployment benefit of £9·20. She has no idea how her benefit is worked out.

All the office jobs that Mrs Browning has applied for have always been taken before she gets a chance of an interview. She feels that £29 gross for a 40-hour week would be a reasonable wage but thinks that she would be too optimistic to expect to get a wage like that. She is registered at the local Employment Exchange but they have not been able to offer her a single job. She has been asked if she would work outside of Liverpool but as she is primarily interested in a part-time job, although she would take full-time work if it was offered, she does not want to go too far as fares would swallow up too much of her wage. Asked if she found the Employment Exchange helpful she replied 'they never say very much'. She relies mostly on the newspaper and her friends to inform her of vacancies.

Although Mrs Browning is not so desperate as some of her neighbours to get work she does feel that the time will come very shortly when her husband's wage will not be sufficient to support them. Like most housewives today, she commented on the steady rise in the cost of living. At the moment she estimates that she spends £20 a week on food, but does not buy very much fresh or cooked meat and adds that coffee is a thing of the past.

Their quarterly gas bill ranged from £12 to £22 in the winter months and their electricity averages about £13 a quarter. Other outgoings include £7·88 a month TV rental, £11·45 a month hire purchase and £5·68 a month on insurance policies. On top of this Mr Brown pays out £6 a month for new car tyres and £22 a month for the car itself. Their house, which is in a reasonable state compared with others in the same road, costs them £3·25 a week rent and rates.

The car is mainly used by Mr Browning for work. He is on call twenty-four hours a day. His normal hours are 6 a.m. to 3 p.m. but some weeks he works longer hours, sometimes as much as seventy-eight a week. He cannot therefore rely too much on public transport. The Brownings only have an evening out together on 'special occasions' which are few and far between. They have no money saved for emergencies and, unless Mrs Browning gets employment, don't expect to be able to afford a holiday next year. Mrs Browning still has many of the clothes she bought when she was employed and has not had to resort to buying secondhand clothes, or using clothing clubs and she hopes that she never will have to.

Mrs Browning doesn't have any time to get bored with her unemployment as she is fully occupied with looking after her young baby and managing the household chores. She does, however, miss the company of other people and the long and unsocial hours her husband works reinforces her feeling of isolation. She is quite hopeful of eventually finding some sort of job, though is not quite so optimistic about the salary she will be able to earn. However, she realises that she couldn't have 'chosen' a worse time to be unemployed and states that she knows that she cannot be choosey in any way about jobs that are offered to her.

Low-wage earner

Mr Daniels has been a road sweeper with the Corporation since mid-1975. Before that he had been out of work for twelve months. He has a wife and four children, all under 11, whom he has to support on his gross wage of £38 a week, plus a weekly guaranteed bonus of £10; he estimates that after deduction he is left with a net weekly wage of £42, plus £4.50 family allowances and 60p family income supplement.

Mr Daniels is caught in a situation where it is difficult for him to decide whether he would be better off financially out of work. Either way he feels he is living on the state. His 60p a week FIS should automatically entitle him to get free school meals for his children, although at the moment he is wrongly charged £3.75, and it will go up to £5 when the fourth child starts school. He considers that his £42 a week is only £4 above the dole, and if he was out of work he would have his rent (£3.25 a week) paid. The family does receive milk tokens for seven pints of milk (they use fifteen a week) but they are anxious about this as they think they will lose their entitlement when Mr Daniels receives a pay increase of £2.50. The family are generally in a state of confusion about what they are entitled to and feel that anyway there is too much red tape involved. In spite of being in work, Mr Daniels feels that their financial situation has deteriorated over the past year. They are still struggling to afford basic necessities. They have cut down on several items of food, although they do try and have two decent meals on Sunday. Mrs Daniels spends £10 on Saturday on food to last them till Tuesday when she spends her £4.50 family allowance on food to last to the end of the week.

The appalling condition of their house causes them to spend about £1 on gas and £2.50 on electricity a week in winter. In common with many other families in the street, they don't use the front room at all because it is so damp, and have bought washable wallpaper for the other rooms to keep the damp out. The damp and the additional burden of having no hot water create severe health hazards for the children and cause Mrs Daniel to get very depressed: 'sometimes I just get up and go out, or else I'd go mad.' They have no running hot water, having to heat water for cleaning, baths and washing clothes. Clothing too has become even more of a problem in the last year. At one time Mrs Daniels had two part-time jobs to help clothe the children, and they used to be able to rely on his parents to give the children clothes at Christmas.

Mr Daniels had hoped to buy a van to do some part-time work in an effort to get extras for the kids, but this is now out of the question as he used up his savings at the time he was out of work, having understood from the local office that since he had savings he was not entitled to supplementary benefit. His period of unemployment has left him distrustful and suspicious of the local social security office. There were always times when benefit payments were delayed and the social security 'always had to be closed'. He felt he would have got more benefit if he 'had been in the know. They don't tell you you can have some savings and still claim benefit. There's no literature around to tell you what you should get. You've got to know the right forms.'

Mr Daniels was also critical of official efforts to help him find a job. There was always encouragement, though not pressure, to go to one of the new development areas, but no real information on what kinds of jobs being offered, what rates of pay, etc. and 'one couldn't afford to chase out there on the off chance.' He seemed to be unaware that he could get his fares from social security. Also he felt there were only 'one or two firms in those areas, such as Courtaulds, and when they decide to pack up you're left with sweet FA.' So Mr Daniels decided to confine his efforts to obtaining a 'safer' job with the Corporation. He found his present job as a road sweeper by persistently going along to the Corporation whenever he heard of a job. The Employment Exchange only sent him after two jobs, and he pursued countless others off his own bat. He didn't find the papers useful either: they were only for skilled workers – 'no one bothers to advertise for labourers – they just go to the nearest street corner.'

His own experience has left him cynical of government training schemes too. After six months' training to be a plasterer he found a job, but lost it three months later when he found he couldn't keep up with more experienced workmates, so he was back to square one. Many other kinds of schemes he says, are creating work for work's sake, which helps neither the unemployed nor the country. 'The money would be better spent on nurseries, which would allow women to go out to work part time. The present system only encourages people to stay on the dole, especially if they have children – in Britain one is definitely penalised for having children. Even a childless couple would need at least £50 a week to make it worth their while to work.'

Wife working, husband unemployed

Mr Sanderson and his wife have recently moved into Liverpool 8. On their marriage, his mother-in-law had bought them a house and previously they lived with his parents-in-law in Speke. Although only 21 Mr Sanderson has had a long stretch of unemployment, since February 1974. Before that, and since leaving school, he had worked continuously with the same firm as a setter operator. His wife still works there, doing the same job, for which she earns £25 to £29 net a week, though as it is piecework it can vary up to £40 gross a week. Out of this she pays a full stamp for herself and her husband. Unemployment came as a harsh blow to Mr Sanderson as he had been with the firm for four years, his wife and two sisters also worked there and although 'the pay wasn't fantastic, at least it was a working wage'. Now he says he wouldn't accept a job at less than £40 gross – which he estimates would give him £28 to £30 net. Although he has been unemployed for so long he is still hopeful of finding work, although he is limited geographically both by his wife's working in the city and because they own their house.

In February 1974, when he became unemployed, Mr Sanderson was living in Halewood and for the first six months he didn't find unemployment too bad as at that time and in that area there were still a few jobs to chase. Also he was receiving both flat-rate and earnings-related unemployment benefit. After six months he moved to Speke and in February 1975, when his unemployment benefit ran out, he received supplementary benefit only, until he married at the end of the year thus losing all right to benefit and becoming dependent on his wife's earnings.

When he was first out of work he attended the Employment Exchange several times a week but has now become disillusioned about its use. 'You hear the same old song. All the jobs have age limits. There seem to be jobs for 15- to 18-year-olds, or otherwise skilled jobs for 25- to 40-year-olds.' He has had eight or nine interviews for various jobs including being a machine operator, general labouring, working in a warehouse, although he has applied for over sixty jobs.

As the prospect of finding a job has gradually diminished, he has found the day becoming endless. He gets up late to save on heating and tries not to eat before midday. He finds it an added strain living off his wife and doesn't feel he can waste her hard-earned money in a pub although he might be missing hearing about possible jobs. He and his wife have almost no social life although they did have one night out recently when she received a small tax rebate. Only lately, since they moved into their house, has he been able to pass the time by doing some brickwork; in general their house looked in better condition than most in the street.

It it difficult for him to gauge whether their standard of living has declined over the past year, as they had been living with his parents-in-law before getting married. They don't have to worry about rent, and they spend between £5 and £8 a week on food; gas and electricity are on meters and cost them 80p a day. They also buy coal costing about £2 a week, and their only other weekly expense is approximately 90p on the launderette.

Single and unemployed

Mr Black is a man in his forties who has been unemployed for two years. From 1947 to 1974 he worked as a refuse collector for the Council before he was laid off sick and consequently lost his job. His income is now made up of £10·23 supplementary benefit and £7 pension from the Council, although when he was first out of work his sick pay came to considerably more. Mr Black lives with his parents who receive retirement and supplementary pension, which includes an exceptional circumstances addition for his mother who is a diabetic.

As is the case with all the families we visited, the family's financial problems are exacerbated by the appalling conditions in which they live. Their continual battle with damp necessitates enormous expenditure on fuel. Their gas is on a meter into which they pay £1 a week; their last quarterly electricity bill was for £26, and since coal went up to £3 they have cut down on that, now spending £1 a week. This fuel expenditure does not include anything for heating water – they have neither hot nor cold and, like the other houses in the street, an outside toilet. In spite of their fuel expenses the Black family's main worry is the price of food. Although they say local shops are very expensive, the cheaper ones are too far away to get to on foot and the cost of transport would wipe out any saving they might make. Even so they say they only spend £6 a week on food.

Since he has been out of work Mr Black has been offered two or three jobs by the Exchange, but did not take them as the rates of pay were too low. He considers that the very lowest net wage he would take would be £25 to £30. On the whole he didn't think the Exchange was very helpful for people of his age: 'at 40 I'm finished – it's more for the youngsters'. Now he relies more on hearing from friends of possible vacancies but he does not hold out much hope of getting work, which is hardly surprising as two of his sisters have husbands who are also unemployed. Others, he says, have been trying to get jobs out of town, but they are finding places are closing down all the time and they are having to come back. What jobs that do come up locally are often only temporary, 'two months at the most and then you're back on the dole'.

One of his neighbours, who had been unemployed for some time, found the burden of having to support a wife and four children on social security overwhelming and actually committed suicide. In spite of there being so much unemployment in the area, he was labelled as a scrounger, although he couldn't get a job which would pay well enough to allow him to support four children. As Mr Black noted, unskilled jobs at decent wages are almost non-existent.

Conclusion

Our detailed studies of the circumstances of some of the people we met further confirm the conclusions we had already reached about life in that part of Liverpool in 1976. To some extent the problems facing the people who took part in our survey, both those in work and the unemployed, were not dissimilar. For example, most of the houses in the two streets were in a bad, and sometimes appalling, condition. Those households with members in employment could, however, sometimes alleviate the conditions. But nevertheless the cost of renovating or adequately heating these houses was extremely high and, given that the majority of those in work were in low-paying occupations, it meant that sacrifices had to be made elsewhere to enable home improvements to be carried out. But the unemployed did not even have the luxury of this choice; the welfare state does not extend its kindness to feeding, clothing and providing money for something which most people would also take for granted, i.e. damp-free rooms.

The bad housing conditions helped to undermine the morale of both the employed and unemployed. But the latter group had other demoralising problems to contend with: the constant job searching and subsequent rejections, the unsympathetic attitude of officials employed by the state to look after the interests of those unable to support themselves through no fault of their own, and the never-ending problem of trying to make ends meet. Making life even more intolerable was the almost universal bafflement over benefit entitlements and the humiliation of having to ask for help. Many of the unemployed could see no immediate end to their problems but, although they were worried about their situation, many accepted it without a feeling that the world had done them an injustice; a few had a vague feeling of 'something better' in the future and clung to this hope. Most were aware that the unemployment crisis in Britain is widespread and recognised that the general economic situation was not totally the responsibility of local official bodies. However, government measures intended to alleviate the problem were criticised.

In no way could any of the unemployed households we met be described as living off the state in a life of luxury. Yet, despite this, there was an undercurrent of feeling amongst the employed that by working a full week themselves and having very little to show for it they were being hard done by, and certain resentments towards their unemployed neighbours were evident to us. This is not suprising as very few of those in work enjoyed a much higher standard of living than those on benefit. Indeed many were also reliant on state benefits themselves. However, the evidence from our study suggests that low wages rather than handsome state pay-outs to the unemployed forced them to live in conditions almost as bad as those out of work.

But even though wages were low and sometimes caused those in work to resent the unemployed, it was clear to us that the majority of the working population, especially those who had experienced a period of unemployment, thought themselves fortunate to have a job. Likewise none of the people out of work gave us the impression that they were enjoying a life of idleness. The monotony and hopelessness of their situation and the lack of an adequate amount of money to live on would, we believe, have been exchanged for a job with a reasonable wage at any time by all of them.

6   The cost of unemployment

Louie Burghes and Frank Field

The comments of some politicians and the media give the impression that unemployment is in some way fundamentally different for the unemployed now compared to the workless of the 1930s. This argument is built on the assumption that the welfare state now provides a fairly generous income for those who are unable to work. In the last chapter we saw what unemployment is like for a small community in Liverpool. The picture that emerged was one of the immense financial, social and emotional costs borne by those who had been denied work in the attempt to control inflation. In this chapter we shall attempt to estimate the cost of unemployment to the unemployed, the cost which unemployment imposes on the taxpayer and the price the community pays for unemployment in the loss of goods and services. We will then be in a position to put a price tag on running the economy at the present level of unemployment.

What is the personal economic cost of unemployment? In answering the question we will first look at the most favourable combination of benefits claimed by only one in five of the unemployed during the first six months of unemployment, and we are therefore judging the extent to which the flat-rate and earnings-related national insurance benefits cushion people in the early stages of unemployment, before going on to examine the income level of the long-term unemployed.

Loss to family

Table 6.1 looks at the incomes of families who have only one breadwinner, first where their breadwinner is employed and then when he or she is unemployed. Later we look at families in which the husband and wife both normally work, but where one of them is unemployed, and see what effect this has on their income. In all the examples we consider a family with both two children and four children and their income after the second week of unemployment and up to the twenty-eighth week (this being the period during which earnings-related supplement can be claimed). The detailed calculations for these tables showing how we arrived at the net weekly spending power are presented in Appendix 1 at the end of the chapter. However, it should be pointed out here that the income of families in which the wife is the unemployed breadwinner is not, in fact, made up of her unemployment benefit and earnings-related supplement alone. The amount to which she is entitled from these benefits falls way below the supplementary benefit level for the family, since a female breadwinner is not entitled to claim unemployment or supplementary benefit for her children and husband. Their income is only brought up to the levels shown in the table if the husband registers for work in order to claim supplementary benefit.

TABLE 6.1 *Net weekly spending power, at November 1976 (£s)*

Family type	Two-child family			Four-child family		
	income level (£)			income level (£)		
	35	55	75	35	55	75
Male breadwinner						
employed	34·37	37·16	48·04	44·83	46·69	58·06
unemployed	30·42	37·16	38·00	40·02	46·11	46·58
Female breadwinner						
employed	36·15	42·10	52·98	44·83	49·47	58·01
unemployed	30·02	30·02	30·02	44·67	44·67	44·67

The one impression which stands out most clearly from the table is the sizeable drop in income which most of the families experience. Only one family would be as well off out of work as in work and only one family actually better off. These exceptions reflect the pitifully low level of child support that is given to families in work. And it is worth emphasising again that not only is this the income that families will receive when the social security benefits are at their most generous but, because of the small percentage of claimants drawing the earnings-related unemployment benefit, only one in five unemployed claimants will be receiving the maximum benefit shown in the table.

An even bigger drop of income occurs for those families who, when the breadwinner becomes unemployed, find themselves ineligible for, or who have exhausted their right to, unemployment benefit. It must seem strange to the families that the system assumes them to need less the longer their period of unemployment. When their entitlement to unemployment benefit is exhausted, the family with the male breadwinner will receive, like the family with the female breadwinner, supplementary benefit of £30·02 for a two-child family and £44·67 for a four-child family. (See Table 6.1, last line) In May 1976, 553,000 unemployed claimants were so poor that they were drawing supplementary benefit. This total constituted a little over 46 per cent of all registered unemployed claimants drawing benefit.

The assumption underlying these figures has been that claimants are eligible during the first six months of unemployment for all the help that is available for them, but only 49 per cent of the unemployed are drawing flat-rate unemployment benefit and a little over 20 per cent of the registered unemployed are claiming any earnings-related supplement. Loss of either of these benefits would have an immediate effect on the net weekly spending power of the families. For example, the two-child family whose gross earnings in work were £55 are credited with an earnings-related benefit of £9 a week. The two-child family with gross earnings of £75 a week may gain an earnings-related supplement of £10·27 a week. We have seen how the income of the unemployed falls again once they are solely dependent on supplementary benefit, a position in which increasing numbers of families whose breadwinner is out of work find themselves, as unemployment rises and the duration of unemployment increases.

Loss of wife's income

We now look at the fall in the family income which results from the loss of employment by a wife, whose husband is also working, and who earned when in work £35, £55 or £75 a week. What Table 6.2 makes clear is that since a married woman is only entitled to a fraction of the unemployment benefit that a married man is entitled to, despite the fact that she may have paid full contributions, the drop in the family income is substantial. The first column in the table below shows the net weekly earnings after tax and national insurance of a married woman at each of the three earnings levels. The first impact on a family when a woman who earns these amounts loses her job is a drop in the family income from her net earnings to her unemployment-benefit entitlement. Again we have calculated the latter on the most generous benefit levels assuming that she does register for work and is eligible to claim both unemployment benefit and earnings-related suplement. When her unemployment benefit and earnings-related supplement entitlement end, the first after twelve months and the second after six, she will not be entitled to any other benefit to compensate for her loss of earnings.

But the same rules do not apply when it is the husband rather than the wife who becomes unemployed. He is entitled to draw the dependants' benefit for his children as well as flat-rate unemployment benefit for himself and earnings-related supplement. But he will only be able to claim benefit for his wife if she is earning less than £8 a week. However once his entitlement to unemployment benefit has run out (after six months for earnings-related benefit and twelve months for flat-rate

TABLE 6.2 *A married woman's earnings in and out of employment at November 1976 (£)*

Employed		Flat-rate unemployment benefit	Unemployed Earnings-related supplement	Total
Gross	Net			
35·00	25·75	9·20	6·32	15·32
55·00	37·60	9·20	9·00	18·20
75·00	49·45	9·20	10·27	19·47

(*Source*: Amounts of ERS payable from *Hansard*, 1976i, cols 247–8)

benefit) the family will be totally dependent on the wife's income.

To sum up: we find that for the vast majority of families, unemployment brings an immediate drop in income even if they are eligible for both the flat-rate and earnings-related unemployment benefit. A further drop in living standards occurs when claimants exhaust their right to national insurance benefits and become dependent on supplementary benefits.

Survey findings

Similar findings on the drop in income which accompanies unemployment are reported in a number of studies on unemployment and redundancy. In her survey of unemployed railwaymen carried out in 1963, Dorothy Wedderburn illustrated the increasing financial problems faced by the longer-term unemployed. She reported that 'At the first interview over half of the total sample employed and unemployed told us that they had not had to cut down on anything.' But a third had reduced expenditure on drink and tobacco, 30 per cent on other items, most often clothes, entertainment and betting. (Wedderburn, 1965, p.152) However, all the families in the sample received a second visit from interviewers ten months later. When these results were analysed, it was found that

> the men without work and with large reductions in earnings had begun to make what were clearly more pertinent and, in some cases, more painful modifications in their spending. Over a third of them had cut down on housekeeping money, in a few cases, by as much as £3 or £5 a week (at the time of the survey this was equal to one sixth of average earnings). There was a real need for economy here.

The study quoted a number of comments from unemployed families.

One family reported, 'we have had to cut down on milk and good cheese, and cuts of meat and buy things that go a long way.' Another family recalled, 'We have a smaller joint, fish and chips are a luxury – no biscuits. Can't afford to bake – buy cheaper tea.' (*ibid.*, p.154) The poverty associated with long-term unemployment is also illustrated in the study Adrian Sinfield carried out on the circumstances of unemployed claimants on Tyneside in 1967. Sinfield found three out of four claimants experiencing a drop in income during unemployment of over 40 per cent, and two in five a drop of over 60 per cent. 'Those living alone or with their family of origin suffered the greatest percentage decline but even among those with children to support fewer than one in six had a drop of less than 20 per cent. (Sinfield, 1970, p.228) Not surprisingly Sinfield went on to report: 'During unemployment all but three households were in poverty by the criteria used in *The Poor and the Poorest* (140 per cent national assistance entitlement plus rent). More than one in three households had an income below their basic national assistance entitlement and one in two were only at the standard level or less than 20 per cent above it.' (*ibid.*, p.228) Judged by these standards, Sinfield observed that it was the unemployed with children who were worse off with over half of this group with incomes below the basic assistance level.

Similar findings emerged from Hill's research, to which we have already referred in earlier chapters. He commented on the small but not insignificant number of families 'falling clearly below the supplementary benefit levels and it is perhaps surprising that about half of them were nevertheless in receipt of supplementary benefit'. (Hill *et al.*, 1973, p.84) In fact the survey, drawn from three boroughs, showed about one in seven of unemployed claimants in this position.

The most recent information on the financial circumstances of the unemployed comes from the national survey conducted by W.W. Daniel (1974). Drawing on the national data Daniel observed

> The cost of unemployment remained substantial for all groups and the idea that the current level of social security benefits for the unemployed made unemployment tolerable was not borne out by our findings. Nearly three quarters (71 per cent) of our respondents said that it had been 'bad' or 'very bad' for them to be out of work. (*ibid.*, p.149)

The national survey also showed that those suffering the greatest costs were workers in the middle age ranges with dependants. Almost 60 per cent of this group had commented that it was 'very bad' to be without work. For most of the unemployed their main concern was lack of money. Of those who said they were concerned about being without work 72 per cent 'spontaneously mention lack of money as the chief reason'. (*ibid.*, p.149) The chief financial problems cited by unemployed claimants in the survey concerned meeting day-to-day living expenses. 'Buying food and clothing for themselves and their children and paying essential bills like the rent, gas and electricity.' (*ibid.*, p.46)

The unemployed and their families in Liverpool, whose views are reported in the previous chapter, made almost identical comments. Mr Green commented upon the demoralisation of unemployment; he and his wife hadn't had an evening out since they were married except for one time when friends paid for them to go to a dance. Mr Sanderson, whose wife is in work, told us of getting up late to save on heating and trying not to eat before midday. The Blacks, whose 40-year old son is now unemployed, gave details of how they have reduced their expenditure on coal from £3 to £1 a week while at the same time pegging the weekly food bills to £6.

In 1971 Dorothy Wedderburn looked at the impact of redundancies at Rolls Royce in Derbyshire. After surveying the evidence she reported,

> The financial hardships of the unemployed may be relative but they are nonetheless real. Moreover, they are accompanied by emotional hardship. The only men who refused to co-operate in a recent study of redundancy were those who had suffered so much that they felt unable to speak of their experience. These feelings tend to be stronger among older men and among those who identify closely with their occupation or place of work. Many blue collar workers doing the most boring jobs miss the structure work gives to their lives: 'Before I used to be able to look forward to the weekend: now every day is the same.' 'It's the feeling you have: the satisfaction of having done a good day's work.' Unemployment involved not only a loss of dignity for the individual: his whole life loses meaning. (Wedderburn, 1971, p.195)

With this thought paramount we turn and examine the costs now placed on the taxpayer and the community which stem directly from denying a large number of working people the right to dignity and self-respect which they can only gain at present from being employed.

Cost to community

Over the past few years researchers have shown that making men idle can be more expensive than keeping them at work (for the first example of this approach see Field, 1971). But no estimate of the overall cost – including loss of national income – has been attempted. To work out the true cost of unemployment we first calculated the loss in direct taxation (we have not been able to estimate the loss in indirect taxation revenue) together with the reduction to the national insurance fund of employees' and employers' contributions. We then went on to examine the amounts paid out to unemployed claimants and their families both from the national insurance fund in the form of flat-rate and earnings-related unemployment benefit, as well as that part of the SBC's budget allocated to the unemployed. As a third stage in calculating the cost of unemployment we collected information on the sums paid out to unemployed persons under the Redundancy Payments Scheme. Lastly, we calculated the loss in output which results from keeping large numbers of persons unemployed. We present the information on each of these counts for each year since 1974, which was an obvious starting point for this analysis. Not only was a new administration elected in February of that year, but we quickly moved to record post-war unemployment, with the Prime Minister and the Chancellor holding out no prospects of a reduction in their numbers in the foreseeable future. The cost of unemployment to the community since 1974 is detailed in Table 6.3. In the Appendix to this chapter the method and sources of calculation for this table are set out in detail.

TABLE 6.3 *Full cost of unemployment in financial years 1974/5, 1975/6 and 1976/7*

Year	Number of unemployed (000)	loss in Tax £m	National insurance fund loss £m		Payment of benefits £m				Loss of output £bn
			Employees' contribs	Employers' contribs	Flat-rate NI benefit	Earnings-related supp.	Supp. benefit	Redundancy payments*	
1974/5	574·3	175	72	47	180	34	190	74	1·22
1975/6	788·3	403	120	134	381	73	330	178	5·71
1976/7	1209	709	225	343	588	112	509	179†	8·03

* calendar years
† January to November

On each of the main counts the cost of unemployment is staggering. We calculate over the past three years a fall in income tax revenue of £1·3 billion. The rise in the numbers of unemployed resulted in a fall of over £940 millions in contributions to the national insurance fund from both employers and employees, while the fund made payments totalling £1·1 billion in flat-rate unemployment benefit and £219 million in earnings-related benefit over the same period. The rise in unemployment from 574,000 in April 1974 to 1,200,000 in April 1976 resulted in claimants making legitimate demands on the SBC amounting to a little over a billion pounds during this period. And on top of this total was a £270 million bill for the administration of benefits to the unemployed. (*Hansard*, 1977g, col. 395) Over £430 million was claimed by unemployed persons from the redundancy payments funds. However the single most important cost to the community of running the economy at a rising level of unemployment comes in loss of national income from keeping large numbers of people idle. We calculate that during 1974 alone, unemployment resulted in a loss of output totalling about £1·2 billion. This rose to £5·7 billion in 1975 and, currently, the loss in output is put at £8 billion. We calculate therefore that over the past three years rising unemployment has resulted in a £15 billion loss in national output. If we can add to this sum the fall in tax revenue and contributions to the national insurance fund, as well as the payment of social security benefits and claims on the redundancy payments fund, the total cost to the community of running the economy at a significantly higher level of unemployment since 1974 is £20 billions.

Conclusion

The cost of unemployment affects all of us. We have shown that its most immediate cost is felt by those who are bearing our unemployment. Most families suffer a significant reduction in net spending power since they have become unemployed, and this drop in income becomes dramatic once unemployment takes on a longer-term nature. But while it is important to keep in mind the individual economic cost, together with the personal costs of unemployment, we also need to focus attention on the cost to the community of running the British economy at a postwar record level of unemployment. In this chapter we have detailed the first ever complete calculation on the cost of unemployment to the community. We have not only looked at the loss in revenue and the payment of social security benefits but, as important, the fall in national income which results from keeping armies of people idle. Rising unemployment since 1974 has cost us as a community very nearly £20 billions.

Why is it that we are prepared to pay such a high price for unemployment? We now turn our discussion to an examination of the main economic argument for running the economy at a record postwar level of unemployment.

Appendix

Notes on Table 6.1. Net weekly spending power in and out of work

Whether the breadwinner is male or female, the assumptions on family composition and household costs are the same.

Two-child family: We have assumed the children to be 4 years old and 6 years old, and the household costs to be: rent £4·72; rates £1·90; work expenses £1·75, and family allowance £1·50. These assumptions are the same as those used by the DHSS. (*Hansard*, 1976i, cols 245–50)

Four-child family: We have assumed the children to be 3, 8, 11 and 16 years old and the household costs to be: rent £5·38; rates £2·18; work expenses, £1·75 and family allowance £4·50. These assumptions are the same as those used by the DHSS. (*ibid.*) The net weekly spending power has been calculated in a similar manner.

Calculating net weekly spending power: The calculations vary depending on whether the husband or wife is the breadwinner. In both cases, the employed are assumed to pay tax and national insurance and to receive, where eligible, rent and rate rebates, family income supplement, free school meals and free welfare milk.

The unemployed are also assumed to receive these benefits where they are eligible. However, a married woman, whether she is the sole breadwinner or not, cannot claim supplementary benefit for her husband and children. The net weekly spending power of the family where the wife is the sole breadwinner and is unemployed is made up not only of her unemployment benefit and earnings-related supplement but, since the latter falls way below the supplementary benefit level, of supplementary benefit paid to the husband for which he has to register for work.

In neither case have we assumed that the family income when out of work has been supplemented by either tax rebates or family income supplement.

On 15 October 1976, the Minister for Social Security said in reply to a Parliamentary Question,

> it is not realistic to regard tax refunds as part of the regular weekly income of an unemployed person since he does not automatically receive these refunds, and when payments are made, they usually occur at monthly intervals. Moreover the payment of tax refunds will depend not only on the point of time in a tax year but also on the number of weeks of employment during the tax year. (*ibid.*, col. 245)

Nor have we included FIS in the calculation of the net weekly spending power of the unemployed. Whether or not families will continue to receive FIS will depend on the time at which the family originally claimed and the time at which they became unemployed. But as FIS is intended to benefit working families, it cannot be considered as income support for the unemployed. Evidence suggests that there are very few unemployed actually receiving FIS. According to Daniel's survey in 1973, only 4 per cent of the unemployed were receiving FIS. (Daniel, 1974) In the first ten months of 1976, approximately 6,000 people had their claim for the renewal of FIS rejected – about a third on the grounds that they were no longer in full-time work. (DHSS, 1975, Table 32.05)

Notes on Table 6.3

The unemployed: We have assumed that all the unemployed are married men with two children and median earnings for male manual workers over 21 years at April each year. (Data from *New Earnings Survey*)

The unemployment figures are for April each year and are taken from the Department of Employment's monthly *Gazette*. The figures used exclude school leavers and adult students.

Tax: As with the unemployment figures the tax figures relate to financial years. The calculations of the tax liability in each year were as follows:

1974 Earnings £41·80, Family Allowance £0·90, Tax Threshold £24·87 Tax at 33 per cent on £17·83 – £5·88

1975 Earnings £53·20, Family Allowance £1·50, Tax Threshold £26·60 Tax at 35 per cent on £28·10 – £9·84

1976 Earnings £62·10, Family Allowance £1·50, Tax Threshold £31·40 Tax at 35 per cent on £32·20 – £11·27

National Insurance Contributions:

1974 *Employer's contribution:* From April until July 1974 the employer's contribution was £1·28 per week per employee. The period was taken to be 18 weeks. From August 1974 until March 1975 the employer's contribution was £1·72 per employee per week. The period was taken to be 34 weeks. For both periods unemployment was taken as being the April level in 1974.

Employee's contribution: From April to July 1974 the employee's contribution was 84p plus 5 per cent on gross earnings above £9·00. From August 1974 until March 1975 the employee's contribution was 75p plus 5 per cent on gross earnings above £9·00.

1975 *Employer's contribution:* During the entire financial year the employer's contribution was 8·5 per cent of gross earnings.

Employee's contribution: The employee's contribution during the same year was 5·5 per cent of gross earnings.

1976 *Employer's contribution:* During the entire financial year the employer's contribution was 8·75 per cent of gross earnings.

Employee's contribution: The employee's contribution during the same year was 5·75 per cent of gross earnings.

Unemployment Benefit: flat-rate, earnings-related and supplementary benefit. Figures for 1974–75 and 1975–76 from *Hansard*, 1976p, cols 321–2. For 1976–77: the cost is based on the assumption that the benefits paid will be no more (or less) expensive in 1976/77 than in 1975/6. In that year unemployment in April was just over 788,000. The total cost of benefits paid to the unemployed in that year was £784 m. We have assumed therefore that the cost per unemployed was in the order of £1,000.

Given an unemployment figure in April 1976 of £1,209,900 we have estimated the cost of unemployment benefits paid to the unemployed in 1976/7 at just over £1·2m.

In 1975/76 the percentage of total benefits paid to the unemployed broke down as follows:

flat-rate unemployment benefit	48·6%
earnings-related unemployment benefit	9·3%
supplementary benefit	42·1%

The costs of each benefit in 1976/77 have been estimated on the assumption that these proportions will be the same in 1976/77 as they were in 1975/76.

Redundancy payments: The figures are taken from a Parliamentary Question, *Hansard*, 1977b, cols 373–4.

Loss of output: The calculation compared the actual output (in terms of GDP) in 1974, 1975 and 1976 with the potential output for these years had the economy grown at its long-run trend rate of growth. We have taken the difference between the actual and potential output as the cost (in terms of loss of output) of the current recession.

To obtain the *long-run trend rate of growth*, we regressed the logarithm of output on the logarithm of time for 1960–73. Output was taken as GDP at factor cost, 1970 prices. The period 1960–73 was chosen because the beginning and end dates represented cyclical peaks in economic activity.

The regression was:

$$\ln y = 32943 + 0.0283 \ln t$$
$$R^2 = 0.99$$

The coefficient of ln t (= 0·0283) is the long-run rate of growth (= 2·83% per annum).

By extrapolating for 1974, 1975 and 1976 we obtained the potential output figures for these years had the economy grown at its long-run trend rate of growth. We compared these potential output figures with the actual output figures for the same years.

| | Output £m | | |
	Potential	Actual	Difference
1974	48·9	48·1	0·8
1975	50·3	47·4	2·9
1976	51·8	48·2*	3·6

From constant to current prices: We used the GDP deflator (current price GDP divided by constant price GDP) to convert these from constant prices to current prices. For 1976 both the current and constant price of GDP had to be estimated.

The GDP deflator for each year is (1970 = 1):

1974 = 1·53
1975 = 1·97
1976 = 2·23

Applying the GDP deflator for each year to the estimated excess of potential output over actual output we obtain an estimate for the cost (in terms of loss of output) of the current recession.

	Excess of potential over actual output (1970 *prices*)	GDP deflator	Loss of output £bn
1974	0·8	1·53	1·22
1975	2·9	1·97	5·71
1976	3·6	2·23	8·03

Estimate of 1976 GDP deflator (i) GDP 1976, constant prices: We took the Treasury 'compromise' forecast of 15 December 1976 for constant price GDP of £47,550m. To obtain an estimate for actual GDP in 1976 we 'corrected' the Treasury 'compromise' forecast by the result of the average of the GDP expenditure data for the first three quarters of 1976 divided by the GDP average estimate for the same three quarters of 1976 at 1970 prices. The correction factor is 1·0129. Our expenditure GDP forecast for 1976 at 1970 prices is therefore: £47550 × 1·0129 = £48163·4m We have used this estimate of 1976 GDP at constant prices for both the GDP deflator and as an estimate of actual GDP in 1976 in calculating the difference between potential and actual output.

(ii) GDP 1976, current prices   To estimate the current price of GDP for 1976 (the Treasury do not publish their forecasts of current price GDP) we have assumed that the increase in the current price of GDP in 1976 over 1975 will be equal to the increase from the second and third quarters of 1975 to the same quarters in 1976. The average increase of these quarters from 1975 to 1976 was 15·44 per cent. Applying that increase to current price GDP in 1975 we obtain an estimate of current price GDP in 1976 of £107550m.

The GDP deflator for 1976 is £107550m (estimate of current price GDP) divided by £48163m = 2·23.

7   What price unemployment?

Chris Pond

Intolerance of high levels of unemployment in this country has been tempered to some extent by the belief that we have a choice between the twin evils of inflation and unemployment. If we could relax our grip on the objective of full employment, it is thought, we might more easily cope with the problem of rapidly rising prices.

In this chapter we consider elements of the debate which has fuelled this belief, itself reflected in public policy towards the unemployed which seems paralysed by this apparent choice. Is there a choice at all? Can we, by allowing the numbers out of work to rise, strengthen our efforts to contain inflation? It is this question to which we now turn.

Inflating the unemployed

Keynesian policies of demand management equipped governments of the 1960s and 1970s with the ability to achieve the objective of full employment. Postwar governments have faced many economic problems, although unemployment was not, until recently, prominent amongst them. The past decade has, however, been characterised by a steady and accelerating increase in the level of unemployment not only in Britain (for details see chapter 2), but throughout the countries of the industrialised world.

This upward trend in unemployment reflected in part not a failure of policies but a failure to use them. The Chancellor of the Exchequer himself admitted in October 1975 that 'to a certain extent the present world recession reflects conscious decisions by individual governments to give priority to restraining inflation and to correcting payment imbalances at the cost of higher unemployment.' (Speech by Rt Hon. Denis Healey, MP, 16 October 1975). As Santosh Mukherjee has pointed out, governments were willing to make this choice because the fear of continuing inflation was greater than that of unemployment – the images of Latin America were stronger than the fading memories of the 1930s (Mukherjee, 1976). Frank Blackaby has also demonstrated how, in Britain, governments' target rate of unemployment shifted upwards throughout the 1960s and 1970s both in terms of the maximum level of unemployment to be tolerated before reflationary action was taken and in the declared objectives of government plans. (Blackaby, 1976).

These decisions, with the consequences which we are now witnessing, were made in the belief that 'a trade-off' was available to governments to choose between different levels of inflation and unemployment: it was thought that a reduction in inflation must involve an increase in the level of unemployment. Given the importance of this belief and its effect on government policy, we need to look more closely at the theoretical foundations on which it is based.

Inflation and unemployment: The theory of a 'trade-off'

The roots of the theory of a trade-off between inflation and unemployment stretch back almost twenty years to the work of A. W. Phillips. Professor Phillips's starting point was the simple proposition that if the demand for a commodity exceeds supply the price will rise, while if supply outstrips demand the price will fall. This, he argued, was no less true of labour than of any other commodity sold on the market. Changes in the price of labour – the wage rate – would be determined by the excess demand for labour (or the excess supply) which Phillips thought would be crudely reflected in the unemployment rate. By plotting the rate of change of money wage rates against the rate of unemployment in each year between the mid-nineteenth century and mid-twentieth century (splitting the period into three) he discovered an apparently resilient relationship between the two – the now well-known Phillips relationship: 'The statistical evidence seems in general to support the hypothesis', he concluded, 'that the rate of change of money wage rates can be explained by the level of unemployment and the rate of change of unemployment.' (Phillips, 1958)

Phillips was satisfied that such a relationship existed, though he was less clear about the reason why – beyond the general proposition that labour behaves in the same way as other commodities to changes in market forces. The pressure of demand might also have its effect through the relative bargaining power of unions and employers or through prices and profits in the product market, all of which tend to inflate or depress the general level of wages depending on the ebbs and flows of market forces.

These simple beginnings laid the foundations for beliefs which still pervade economic thought and, more important, public policy. The implications of Phillips's analysis was that, for any given level of unemployment, there is an associated rate of price increase. A lower level of unemployment will be accompanied by a higher rate of inflation (price rises fuelled by wage rises). Phillips himself estimated that (assuming a 2 per cent annual increase in productivity) a rate of unemployment of about 2·5 per cent would be needed to maintain stable *prices* or of 5·5 per cent to maintain stable *wage rates*. This kind of exercise has ever since fascinated economists: Paish, for example, estimated that during the 1960s inflation was the inevitable result of reducing the unemployment rate below about 2·25 per cent. (Paish, 1968) The actual level throughout the period 1955–66 averaged only 1·5 per cent. Estimates of the unemployment rate necessary for price stability in the early 1970s have been put as high as 5 per cent. (See Burton, 1972) It is perhaps because of these fundamental social and political implications that the Phillips relationship has attracted so much academic interest. The argument suggests that the objective of full employment can only be achieved 'at a price' and that price is inflation.

A dying relationship

No sooner had the Phillips relationship been brought into the light of day than economists began updating the research and applying it to other countries with enthusiasm. The results were, however, disappointing. While the relationship seemed to be quite strong for the late-nineteenth and early-twentieth centuries, any association seemed to have evaporated when applied to other countries or to the postwar data on wage rates and unemployment in Britain. Faced with the prospect that this important finding may have become obsolete as soon as it had been discovered, many set about constructing variations on the same theme. Researchers found that if they used alternative variables (earnings instead of wage rates, or vacancy statistics as well as unemployment figures for instance) and if they made allowances for the shortcomings of the published data (for example by estimating the level of 'hidden' unemployment) the relationship could be revived. The model was also bent and twisted to take account of other factors which the original simple theory had ignored, but which were stubbornly relevant in reality. Hence the effect of the business cycle, of price changes, of trade unions, profits and of wage-price or wage-wage spirals were all grafted onto the original simple hypothesis.

The theory suffered a further, almost critical, setback when, in the late 1960s and early 1970s it became clear that high rates of unemployment were failing to have the expected depressive effect on either the increase in wage rates or price rises: in many countries rapid inflation and high unemployment were beginning to cohabit. In Britain the so-called 'wage explosion' of the early 1970s took place against a background of the highest level of unemployment experienced since the war. Unemployment continued to rise even under policies which held back the increase in money-wage rates and thereby, some hoped, to improve the terms of the 'trade-off' (giving a lower increase in money wages for each level of unemployment). In fact, recent incomes policies have served as a vivid demonstration of the implausibility of the supposed relationship between unemployment and inflation. Such policies have effectively held wage increases *below* the rise in the cost of living – yet both inflation and unemployment have continued to rise.

One might reasonably have expected that in the face of such evidence the Phillips relationship would have been laid to rest. The explanation that recommends itself is that if the relationship had applied to earlier historical periods – perhaps in the Victorian and Edwardian era of free competition and before the development of institutionalised labour markets – conditions had now changed. Even Phillips himself warned that the relationship would not hold under pressure of rapidly rising import prices. (Phillips, 1958) Nor could the theory readily cope with the possibility of increasing structural unemployment unrelated to the aggregate level of domestic demand and wage rates.

Despite these setbacks, the theory of a trade-off between unemployment and inflation still maintains a firm grip on some sections of economic thought and public policy. How can the highest rate of inflation together with the highest levels of unemployment experienced in the postwar period be reconciled with a theory which argues a trade-off between the two?

Some proponents of the theory argue that these developments are not inconsistent with the existence of a trade-off but that the terms of that trade-off have merely deteriorated. The case explained by Sam Brittan contains three elements: the meaning of the unemployment figures, the importance of price expectations, and the role of trade unions. Brittan begins with the argument that the unemployment figures have changed their true meaning – that one million unemployed in the mid-1970s is not the same thing as one million unemployed in the mid-1960s or the mid-1950s. The argument runs that because of legislative changes which have 'softened' the impact of unemployment for individuals the costs of 'job search' and voluntary unemployment have been reduced. This implies two things. First, that at any one time the unemployment register will indicate a higher than true level of unemployment. In chapter 1 we have already shown that this view does not stand up to careful examination and we need not pursue the argument here, except to remind readers that the true level of unemployment is probably much higher than the register indicates. Second, the argument of higher voluntary unemployment implies that workers face a lower cost of 'job-search'. They can therefore afford to be out of work for a longer period of time while waiting for a higher wage, and this exerts an upward pressure on wage rates overall. We will return to the flaw in this argument in due course.

As Brittan readily admits, however, it would be stretching this line of argument too far to suggest that the unemployment register was now moving in the opposite direction to the true level of unemployment. Although the official figures may overstate the real unemployment level (according to this argument) the actual rise in the numbers out of work cannot be denied altogether. This leads to the second line of reasoning in defence of the theory: that the trade-off remains, but that the terms of the trade-off have worsened. In other words, each level of unemployment is now associated with a higher rate of inflation than before. This worsening of the trade-off is attributed to two factors: the development of inflation-consciousness amongst work people and the increasing power of trade unions. We will take each of these in turn.

Perhaps one of the most prominent proponents of the first explanation is Milton Friedman. Friedman argues that a 'natural unemployment rate' exists which is independent of the rate of inflation. This is determined by the industrial resources, technology, labour skills, enterprise and so on with which the economy is endowed at a given point in time. Attempts by governments to push the level of unemployment below this level will only be successful in the short run. In the longer term such efforts will be rewarded with still higher rates of inflation. The economy will then drift back to the natural (or 'equilibrium') level of unemployment. According to this view, the long run 'Phillips curve' is not a 'curve' at all in the ordinary sense, but a vertical line which is theoretically consistent with *any* level of inflation. Demand management policies may have some effect in reducing unemployment if it is above that level, but below this point demand stimulation will only result in inflation.

Of fundamental importance to this theory is the role of price expectations. The economists who forward these views believe that people's actions are determined not by their *money* wage – as Phillips believed – but by their *real* wage (after taking account of inflation). They argue therefore that Phillips's relationship between *money* wages and unemployment could only hold in the short term, while the rate of price increase was small (so that money wages and real wages were very much in line) and while wage earners wore the blinkers of 'money illusion' – not realising that the purchasing power of their wage was falling. Once people have overcome this handicap they begin to take price rises into account in their wage demands, and once they have experienced a steady rate of inflation for a period they also begin to anticipate wage rises in the future.

Following this line of argument, therefore, attempts by governments to maintain a lower level of unemployment by allowing wage rates to rise at a steady pace will result in inflation. This level of inflation will be built into wage demands which will themselves be reflected in higher prices. Unemployment will then drift back to its 'equilibrium level' and inflation will be higher than before. For each level of unemployment there will be a higher level of price increases. Of course trade unions may have a vital role to play in this process by helping their members to overcome 'money illusion'. But the 'new theorists' of the inflation–employment trade-off see another, more sinister, way in which trade unions have turned the rules of the game against the economic good of the nation.

Early proponents of the Phillips relationship discounted the effects of trade unions on the relationship between unemployment and wage rates, treating them merely as a 'rubber stamp' to the wage determination process. Unions were seen merely as one element of collective bargaining – as an instrument rather than as an influence. Thus it was argued that unions could not, in aggregate, affect the actual level of wages, which were determined by demand for labour. The level of demand could, of course, affect the strength of trade unions at the bargaining table. Evidence presented by A. G. Hines showed that changes in money wages could be as easily correlated with the level and changes in union membership as with unemployment. (Hines, 1964) But this presented little problem for the theory: when demand for labour is high, it was argued, trade union membership can be expected to rise; when it is low, people will become unemployed and unions will lose members.

The new proponents of the 'inflation–employment trade-off' have brought trade unions back into the picture as an additional explanation for the coexistence of high rates of unemployment and inflation. The unions, it is argued, do not allow the wages of their members to react to the normal pressure of market forces. Rather, they act as monopolists controlling the supply of labour who force wages beyond a level consistent with moderate (perhaps 'natural') levels of unemployment. At the same time, they perform in a 'quasi-political' manner to ensure that the higher wages demanded are paid under threat of a strike and that the monetary and fiscal authorities pursue policies which accommodate such demands. The inevitable result once more, it is said, is higher rates of inflation associated with each level of unemployment.

These are the bones of the argument behind the belief that 'acceptable' price stability requires the sacrifice of full employment. As John Burton has argued, 'whichever way the government jumps, it threatens to be impaled on one of the horns of this dilemma, and the end in either case may well be electoral suicide.' (Burton, 1972, p. 71) We should remember that the implications of this argument stretch further than the academic debate. The belief that such a dilemma exists is clearly at the heart of public policy towards the unemployed and fear of being 'impaled on one of the horns of the dilemma' has had the effect of apparently paralysing governments from taking decisive action on the unemployment problem.

The counter-attack

This view of the causes and solutions of inflation can be criticised on a
number of grounds. First, it has been shown that none of the 'trade-off'
models based on the Phillips relationship, including the most recent
adaptations which include the role of price expectations, actually
conform to the most recent data. (Henry, Sawyer and Smith 1976)
Second, one could point to their limited usefulness as *positive* guides to
policy (as opposed to negative constraints on action). As Frank Blackaby
has pointed out, the proponents of this view have a rather unsatisfactory
message for politicians: 'If you continue to raise the level of
unemployment, at some point, we don't know where, the rate of rise in
earnings will begin to moderate. You will then have to keep
unemployment at this unknown point for an unknown period of time,
and you will then be able to bring it down again to an unknown figure.'
(Blackaby, 1976, p. 287) The theory therefore offers little precise guidance
for policy-makers. Indeed, its existence may well contribute to the
pursuit of policies which themselves accelerate the trend to increased
unemployment and inflation. For instance, one school of thought argues
that increased taxation throughout the 1960s was the orthodox Treasury
response to balance-of-payments deficits and inflation. The aim was to
restrict effective demand and consumption, thereby releasing resources
for exports and productive investments. But the corporate sector failed
to take up the resources released from consumption (partly no doubt
because deficient domestic demand does not encourage firms to invest).
The result, it is argued, was a government surplus which generated
increased unemployment, together with the stimulation of cost-plus
inflation through a wage-tax spiral. (Wilkinson and Turner, 1975)
Similarly, Frank Blackaby argues that governments' abilities to combat
both inflation and unemployment are substantially increased with an
incomes policy. Such policies have proved themselves most successful
when they have the cooperation of the trade union movement. Such cooperation is, however, placed under great stress if governments continue
at the same time to pursue policies of trying to reduce inflation by
allowing unemployment to rise. Finally, one can demonstrate the
inconsistency of the theory when compared with present economic
reality

Essentially, the 'trade-off' theories are based on a relationship between
unemployment and changes in wage rates. From there the proponents
take the rather doubtful step of equating increases in domestic wage
rates with inflation. The debate as to whether trade unions 'cause
inflation' is a complex and wide-ranging one on which we cannot
embark here. For our present purposes we need only point to some
aspects of the economic situation to throw doubt on the validity of this
assumption. First, it is valuable to note that since 1974, when increasingly

stringent wages policies have slowed the increase in wage rates and earnings to a level well below the increase in prices, inflation and unemployment have continued to escalate. Second, the facts allow little scope for the belief that the present inflation is generated by domestic pressures (let alone by domestic wage increases). Such a belief must ignore the existence of high rates of unemployment and inflation throughout the advanced industrial world in the late 1960s and 1970s; it must ignore the influence of the very large increases in the prices of imported raw materials (especially oil) and finished products and the effect on domestic prices of Britain's entry to the EEC; and it must also discount the very real effects of exchange rate changes which have recently exacerbated Britain's inflationary problems. Such a belief can only be said to be clinging to a theoretical framework regardless of reality.

Much of the present inflationary problem, therefore, must be attributed to forces outside the British economy. Nevertheless, in the early 1970s there was said to be a 'wages explosion' which many still believe contributed greatly to the acceleration of domestic price inflation. Again in 1974, with the reintroduction of free collective bargaining under the social contract, the level of wage increases rose substantially, lending support to the view that Britain's inflationary problems originated at the wage-bargaining table. Evidence has since shown that in neither of these periods was the apparently high level of money wage settlements sufficient to offset the contemporary rise in prices and tax deductions. In terms of real net earnings, the spending power of wage earners probably increased only marginally, if at all, during these periods. (See Wilkinson and Turner, 1975 and Pond, Field and Winyard, 1976) Thus the increases could have contributed little to consumer spending, although they could of course have had their effects on labour costs. How successful is the strategy of allowing unemployment to rise as a defence against this type of inflationary pressure?

Whose unemployment?

In Chapter 2 we showed that unemployment is by no means evenly distributed amongst all members of the work force. Those at the beginning or end of their working lives, women and coloured workers, the unskilled, all carry a heavieer burden of the total level of unemployment. Are these the people at the heart of Britain's inflationary problems? Has unemployment successfully rooted out the villains of the piece? The evidence suggests not.

Certain groups are consistently more vulnerable in the labour market:

these same groups who we can identify as having higher rates of unemployment are also those more likely to be low paid, to be in jobs where there are poor working conditions, little training facilities, and high staff turnover. Material in Chapter 2 warns against confusion between association and causation when considering which groups figure prominently amongst the unemployed. The same argument applies to the low-pay problem – these groups do not 'cause' low pay any more than they cause unemployment; they are merely the victims of these problems.

Nevertheless, many have been led to argue that rewards in the labour market reflect differences in the productive potential of individuals – differences associated with peoples' holdings of 'human capital'. Why then, should it be that women and coloured workers tend to reap lower rewards than their male or white counterparts regardless of the level of education or training; why also should a man in his fifties, perhaps with a lifetime of training and experience behind him, find it more difficult to get a job than a man in his thirties without these attributes? Outside of a narrow range of occupations requiring physical strength, the human capital explanations provide no satisfactory answer.

Realisation of this dilemma has brought many economists to the conclusion that there is not one labour market (as assumed in the debate on the Phillips relationship) but at least two, and maybe more. The proponents of this view argue that two types of occupations can be identified. On the one hand, there are those which are characterised by high wages, good working conditions, job security, extensive on-the-job training and low staff turnover. All these characteristics, they point out, tend to go together. At the other extreme are firms with low wage levels, poor working conditions, job instability, little training provision and high staff turnover. Jobs with these bundles of good or bad characteristics may exist side by side within any sector of industry or even within the same firms. The effect, however, is to create two distinct labour markets. How can this be explained?

The theorists argue that firms and organisations themselves fall into two types: first, there are those with fairly rigid occupational hierarchies – jobs in these organisations are well-defined and require specific skills. To create a work force with the appropriate skills, such firms may undertake extensive on-the-job training. This equips staff both to do their own jobs and, when vacancies occur, to move into other jobs higher up the ladder which could not be filled by people from outside the organisation without the specific skills needed. These organisations therefore recruit new people at the bottom of the job ladder only, with higher-level jobs being filled by existing staff. The prevailing level of unemployment will affect the standards demanded by such organisations when taking on new recruits at the bottom of the jobs ladder. But once inside, the door is slammed against the winds of economic change. The economic climate in the external labour market is no longer relevant. (Doeringer and Piore, 1971) These firms, having committed themselves to expenditure in training their staff will wish to discourage turnover and encourage a commitment to the organisation. If staff leave, this shortens the pay-off period of the training investment and the firm will have to begin again. They will therefore provide good wages and working conditions as well as good prospects for promotion within the organisation. Such firms will also be wary when recruiting new staff to ensure that they have the characteristics associated with stability: their choice in this may well be determined by discrimination of an ethnic sort (refusing to take on coloured workers or women) or of a statistical nature (refusing to take on members of groups *thought* to be prone to high turnover). (Gordon, 1972)

This sector constitutes the 'core' or 'primary' labour market, populated by certain categories of workers (mainly men between their mid-twenties and fifties who do not belong to ethnic minorities and who have some level of specific skills). The 'secondary' market represents the opposite side of the coin; jobs requiring no specific skills and therefore offering no on-the-job training; since firms have not 'invested' in their work force, there are no costs involved in high staff turnover, which may even be encouraged; there is no need, therefore, to try and ensure that workers stay with the firm by paying wages at a high level, providing job security, good conditions or the possibility of advancement. By and large it is those workers who have been excluded from the primary labour market (because of their labour force characteristics) who find themselves in such jobs.

The two labour markets may exist side-by-side in the same firms. As we have seen, firms who have invested in training of their staff will not necessarily be willing to relinquish that investment, even if demand is slack. Planning for the long term, firms will be more likely to 'hoard' such labour until the economy picks up again. But this need not be true of their whole labour force and certain groups of workers may be employed in jobs requiring relatively few skills who are easily disposable. Such workers may act as a valuable 'buffer' against the extremes of excess and insufficient demand – when business is slack, such workers are easily discarded at little cost to firms; when the economy picks up they are easily recruited again in the external labour market. Evidence presented by Nicholas Bosanquet and P. B. Doeringer show this to be true of coloured workers employed in the Yorkshire woollen industry who 'were first hired when the production day lengthened, when shift working was introduced or in other circumstances when the companies were having difficulty recruiting white labour at the going rate.' (Bosanquet and Doeringer, 1973)

Those who are only taken on during an upswing, we may expect, will also be the first to go when market conditions deteriorate. Similar evidence presents itself for industries such as retailing which depend to a large extent on women, part-timers and school leavers. These groups are not often provided with much training and are therefore easily dispensable should labour costs have to be cut. As Anthony Giddens has argued, long-term planning of labour supply involves firms in substantial costs so that 'employers may be expected to complement their long-term labour investment with a pool of highly "disposable" labour, in which a marked degree of labour turnover may be tolerated or even encouraged.' (Giddens, 1973, p. 220)

This high labour turnover, characteristic of the secondary labour market, may be accepted by both sides when employment prospects are healthy. Workers in 'dead-end' and low-paying occupations are likely to have little commitment to their jobs and stability is not encouraged or rewarded. Job changing may therefore be frequent amongst secondary market workers. This itself helps to reinforce the polarisation of the two markets since workers with a 'chequered' employment history are unlikely to be considered as suitable recruits to primary jobs.

As Adrian Sinfield has argued 'The tactic of frequent job changing may serve to ease the boredom and constraints of the many dead-end jobs available to unskilled youths, but with high or increasing unemployment, such "games turn deadly".' (Sinfield, 1976, p. 240)

In a recession, those groups most prone to high turnover are obviously more likely to find themselves amongst the unemployed. Proponents of the trade-off theory, however, argue that such job changing is merely the rational response of people looking for better paid or more suitable employment – hence a large number of the unemployed are voluntarily so. Indeed, some argue that this process of job-search provides the mechanism through which wage rates respond to the level of unemployment. The wage aspirations of those in and out of work vary according to the level and therefore the expected duration of unemployment. (See Holt, 1969)

In our discussions in Chapter 2 we have seen that the current unemployment problem is not characterised by short-term unemployment, as we might expect if a large part of the total represented voluntary job-searching. But even if this view of the unemployment problem were correct, how could one explain the greater numbers of women, young workers, immigrants and older workers amongst the unemployed. Why, as Hines has pointed out, 'should women, according to the interpretation which the theory would invite us to put on the data, be more "rational" than men, and black women more so than white women? ... why as compared to whites should blacks be better neo-classical optimisers ...?' (Hines, 1976) As soon as we begin to look carefully at the unemployment problem, the elegant models on which public policy is based begin to appear tarnished by reality.

The dual-labour-market approach helps to explain the unequal distribution of the unemployment problem. If it is correct it has important consequences for public policy, especially regarding the unemployment–inflation trade-off. Such a theory allows us to focus on the effects of pursuing a policy of higher unemployment to restrain the rate of inflation. The image we see through this microscope is of one sector of the economy where wages are high and strength in the labour market relatively great. *If* there is an inflationary pressure of wage demands, or – more likely – an ability to maintain real wages, it is in this sector that it is to be found. But those who are lucky enough to inhabit the primary labour market are not those most likely to carry the burden of unemployment when it strikes. Jobs in this sector are relatively secure.

W. W. Daniel and E. Stilgoe have argued that unemployment has tended to increase independently of the general level of demand in the economy, a phenomenon which they explain as a growing mismatch between the characteristics of the unemployed and those demanded in available vacancies. (Daniel and Stilgoe, 1976) This being so, we must realise that the supposed trade-off between inflation and unemployment will become increasingly ineffective. There will be more than ever a need to stop regarding unemployment as an instrument of economic policy, and to begin treating it as the severe social problem that it is.

Conclusion

Throughout the Western industrialised world, governments in the late 1960s committed themselves to a fundamental decision which involved the abandonment of full employment as the prime objective of economic policy. They did this in the belief that such a decision would allow them to control the increasing inflationary pressures which were then building up and which posed a seemingly greater threat than that of unemployment. This decision involved a tragic miscalculation, based on a relationship thought to exist for which there is little evidence. The costs of this miscalculation have been high, borne by the most vulnerable groups who are experiencing more than their fair share of the highest level of unemployment in the postwar period.

If the Phillips relationship ever existed it could only apply to the level of domestic wage increases which, the evidence suggests, is not the prime cause of the current inflation. But even here, the theory of a trade-off is based on an oversimplified view of the labour market. By arguing in terms of aggregate unemployment and aggregate wage increases, the theorists – and the governments who have followed their teaching – have missed the fundamental point that unemployment does not necessarily strike at the sectors in which the pressures for wage increases originate. To a large extent, strength in the labour market to demand excessive wage increases is also reflected in job security.

At some level of unemployment no doubt, the wage aspirations of even the strongest groups will be tempered. But it is likely to be at such a level that governments will consider it an unacceptable price to pay, even for the attainment of price stability. How unacceptable is the price which is being paid by the unemployed is one of the main issues to emerge from the next chapter.

8 Causes of unemployment

Steve Hannah

As we have seen in Chapter 2, the level of unemployment has been increasing in leaps and bounds since 1966. What has caused such an unprecedented rise? The orthodox thinking is that this has occurred because of higher welfare benefits and excessive wage claims. We have shown in earlier chapters that there is little substance in these arguments. This chapter considers the relevant arguments in more detail and examines other reasons why well over a million people are still unnecessarily out of work.

The long-term movement of unemployment and vacancies, depicted in Figure 8.1, illustrates three important features of the labour market. First, unemployment and vacancies tend to rise and fall in a cyclical manner. Second, even when the labour market appears to be at its 'tightest' (that is when unemployment is relatively low and vacancies are relatively high) there still exists a substantial amount of unemployment. Finally, since 1966, a significant change in unemployment behaviour has occurred. Cyclical fluctuations have become more pronounced, particularly since 1971, and the average level of unemployment has risen substantially. The effect of this change has been to raise unemployment rates to unprecedented postwar levels. Figure 2.1 in Chapter 2 illustrated the unemployment rates during four complete postwar cycles and clearly shows that even before 1965 there was a slight upward tendency in the average rate of unemployment. However, since 1965 there has been a sharp and almost continuous rise in unemployment which has only been interrupted by the short-lived 'Barber boom' of 1972/3.

Types of unemployment

Analyses of the causes of unemployment traditionally identify two main types of unemployment: that due to a deficiency in aggregate effective demand and that due to structural and institutional factors. In addition, reference is often made to whether workers are either voluntarily or involuntarily unemployed. Although this distinction has many

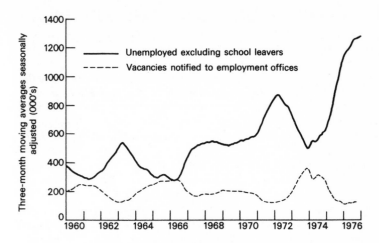

FIGURE 8.1 *Unemployment and vacancies in Great Britain, 1960–76*

theoretical advantages it is particularly difficult to apply in practice. (For a discussion of this point see Worswick, 1976 especially Chapter 1.)

Demand-deficient unemployment is associated with the Keynesian analysis of effective demand and is said to exist when, given the existing level of wages and prices, the aggregate demand for labour falls short of the available supply. This type of unemployment varies with the movements of the trade cycle, which constitutes the periodic rises and falls in consumers' expenditure, exports and investment – the three main components of aggregate demand. The resultant loss of jobs is generally considered to be beyond the control of the individual worker and it corresponds to what Keynes defined as 'involuntary' unemployment.

The second type of unemployment arises from the combination of many factors and is related to the institutional and structural features of the labour market. Within this category, four groups of unemployed workers are often identified. The groups are not mutually exclusive and their main purpose is to identify the particular economic forces at work. It would not be possible for instance to categorise individual workers. The first group of workers are those who have just entered the job market or who are between jobs (frictional or short-term unemployment). This type of unemployment, usually of a short-term nature, is bound to exist even when the economy is at full stretch, and mirrors the inevitable (but not immutable) imperfections in a decentralised labour market. 'Full employment' is therefore quite consistent with the existence of this type of unemployment and indeed the latter probably increases when the economy expands as more workers voluntarily leave their jobs to try and take advantage of a market which is in their favour. This type of unemployment can also increase if workers take a longer time in order to find another job. Second, there are those workers who are said to have become unemployed because of strong trade unions demanding excessively high wages. Although, to the individual worker, this type of unemployment may appear involuntary, it is often considered voluntary as it results from the conscious decision of a collection of individual workers, that is, a trade union. The third group of workers consists of those who, although registered as unemployed, are not really part of the labour market at all. These are the so-called 'unemployables' – a very small minority of the unemployed who comprise the old, the sick, the disabled and the workshy. These are society's rejects, who would be unemployed whatever the state of aggregate demand. Finally, there are some workers who are unemployed for longer periods of time because of certain structural imbalances in the economy (structural unemployment). This type of unemployment also arises from demand deficiencies, not in the aggregate, but in particular industries and regions. The long-term decline in the shipbuilding, textile and coal industries, the concentration of economic activity in particular regions of the country, and increasing automation and technological advance have all been important contributory factors to this type of unemployment. Such changes have meant that certain skills and crafts are no longer required or that certain areas or regions have become subject to economic 'blight'. It takes time for workers and industry to adjust to such fundamental changes and unemployment of a more long-term nature is an understandable result.

These traditional classifications therefore suggest that unemployment exists for a large number of reasons which may vary from time to time in their relative importance. It is clearly essential to realise which causes are predominant at any particular moment if correct policies are to be followed. For instance, the remedy for demand-deficient unemployment would normally entail the government boosting expenditure via deficit financing – a conventional Keynesian technique. This remedy, however, would be quite inappropriate if most unemployment was of the non demand-deficient type. In this case, deficit-financing would largely lead to inflation with little reduction in unemployment. This type of unemployment requires quite different measures. A reduction in frictional unemployment might necessitate, for instance, an improvement and enlargement of the services provided by Employment Exchanges and Job Centres. As a result people would find a new job much quicker and with greater ease and would thus be unemployed for a much shorter time. In the case of 'excessive' wage claims a rigorous incomes policy might be called for. For the so-called 'unemployables' the most appropriate measures would be rehabilitation facilities and sheltered employment schemes. Structural unemployment, however, calls for selective regional measures, for re-training facilities and for assistance to workers in moving from areas of high to areas of low unemployment.

In addition, it is necessary to identify the main influences giving rise to unemployment in order to assess the importance of 'full employment' as a policy target *vis-à-vis* other policy targets such as a stable price level, industrial growth and a strong balance of payments. For instance, if a large rise in unemployment occurred because of voluntary factors, then policy-makers might well assign the return to 'full employment' a lower priority than if the increase had been due to involuntary forces.

Having briefly reviewed the main concepts used to explain the existence of unemployment, we now consider their application to the current employment situation. We have already noted the significant increase in unemployment since 1966. Is the explanation to be found in demand-deficiencies, or are structural and institutional factors the main influence at work? Moreover, is the increase largely represented by a rise in voluntary unemployment or not? The former question is often posed in terms of whether the 'full employment' level of unemployment has substantially increased. Before we discuss the various attempts which have been made to quantify this 'minimum' level of unemployment we turn to a consideration of the concept of full employment.

Concepts of full employment

We have already seen that some degree of unemployment remains even when the economy appears to be working at full capacity. The concept of full employment is usually quantified in terms of the size of this 'minimal' level of unemployment. There have been three main approaches to defining the concept of capacity and hence of full employment.

The first is in terms of what policy-makers consider to be an 'acceptable' level of unemployment given that they have other economic objectives. The implication is that there is a conflict between the goal of full employment and other policy targets such as a stable price level and a balance-of-payments surplus. The level of unemployment associated with this definition of full employment would thus be determined by the preferences of policy-makers and would represent an 'optimum' level in the sense of being consistent with a package of desired policy targets.

One way of measuring this type of full employment is to consider the occasions on which a government takes rapid reflationary measures because it obviously considers the level of unemployment too high. This method suggests unemployment rates of 2·0, 2·2 and 3·6 per cent in 1958, 1962 and 1971 respectively. (Figures quoted by Blackaby, 1976, p. 281. They relate to the United Kingdom and exclude school leavers and adult students.) The government's present reluctance to reflate implies a figure even higher than 3·6 per cent. Alternatively, target figures of full employment can be derived or estimated from the various economic plans. This approach yields figures of 1·5, 1·5 and 1·6 per cent from plans published in 1963, 1965 and 1969 respectively. (*ibid.*, p. 282) The last figure appears to be on the low side considering the rates of unemployment that were actually tolerated between 1967 and 1970.

From this evidence it is clear that the target rate of unemployment has risen substantially since the 1960s. However, this does not necessarily mean that there has actually been a significant structural change in the labour market. The change may just reflect a switch in official assessments of the social costs and benefits of running the economy with a high level of employment. Whether this realignment can be justified in terms of the actual behaviour of the economy still remains to be seen. Indeed, a fundamental assumption underlying this approach is that there exists a trade-off between unemployment and inflation. As we have already shown, in Chapter 7, there is little evidence to substantiate this claim.

The second approach to defining full employment is associated with the monetarist school of economic thought and its theory of the natural rate of unemployment. The high priest of monetarism, Professor Milton Friedman, has defined the natural unemployment rate as follows:

> At any moment of time, there is some level of unemployment which has the property that it is consistent with equilibrium in the structure of real wage rates .... The 'natural rate of unemployment', in other words, is the level that would be ground out by the Walrasian system of general equilibrium equations, provided there is imbedded in them the actual structural characteristics of the labour and commodity markets, including market imperfections, stochastic variability in demands and supplies, the cost of gathering information about job vacancies and labour availabilities, the costs of mobility and so on. (Friedman, 1968, p. 8)

The monetarist theory argues that full employment exists when real wages are stable and when all inflation is fully anticipated. In the long term the government cannot reduce the natural rate by traditional demand-management methods without generating an accelerating rate of inflation.* Academic monetarists have made several attempts to

---

*In describing the natural unemployment rate David Laidler argues that, 'It would however, be independent of the inflation rate, and thus would not be susceptible to being altered by orthodox Keynesian, macro-economic "demand management" policies. Only in the short run would an expansion of aggregate demand lead to reduced unemployment. In the long run the only effect would be to raise the inflation rate ... ' (Friedman, 1975, p. 45)

calculate the level of 'natural' unemployment in this country and the more reliable estimates suggest a rate of just under 2 per cent. (NIESR, 1977, p. 48) However, the political sympathisers of monetarism have implied that the rate is much higher, arguing that even the currently high level of unemployment cannot be significantly reduced without generating another period of increased inflation.

There have been many theoretical objections to the natural-rate hypothesis, some of which have been discussed in Chapter 7. In particular, it can be shown that perfectly anticipated inflation is quite consistent with substantial involuntary unemployment. (Trevithick, 1976) During the depression of the 1930s there can be no doubt that the very low rate of inflation was fully anticipated but that substantial unemployment of a very 'unnatural' kind existed.

The third definition of full employment is that of Keynes and is said to exist when involuntary unemployment is zero. According to Keynes involuntary unemployment exists because of deficiencies in aggregate demand and any remaining unemployment must be of the frictional, structural or voluntary type. In terms of assessing the social costs of unemployment and of appraising structural changes in the labour market this definition has the most immediate relevance and further discussion in this chapter of full employment will generally be referring to the Keynesian concept. We now turn to our original question of whether the level of unemployment associated with full employment has actually increased or not and, in particular, whether the increase is largely due to voluntary factors.

The classical theory revisited

A view which has found increasing popular support is that the rise in unemployment since 1966 is largely voluntary and does not have the same welfare implications as unemployment did in earlier years. We have examined the relevant arguments in Chapter 3. As a summary the following extract illustrates clearly the flavour of the argument – it was written at the time when unemployment reached the 'magic' level of $1^1/_2$ million in 1976.

> A great deal of unemployment today is the product of Government actions designed to win union support and make middle-class parliamentarians feel virtuous. The earnings related unemployment benefits, social security payments and redundancy payments have long reduced the need for people to get off the dole queues in a hurry. (*Daily Telegraph*, 25 August 1976)

The 'cushioning process' of welfare benefits is therefore seen to be the main factor behind the steep increase in the figures of registered unemployment. Another facet of the theory is the argument that excessive wage claims in recent years have priced workers out of their jobs;

> given that no conceivable economic system can ensure that everybody works, unemployment over and above the natural level (that determined by the fact that some do not want to work, others cannot, and that no conceivable non-totalitarian system can ensure that every able-bodied person works) is caused by trade unions and by trade unions alone. When a trade union demands a wage increase which the market – or the financial resources of a given firm or industry – cannot bear either the increase can be paid to fewer people – a number being made redundant – or what is available is shared out between the existing work force, or the firm goes bankrupt. (*Spectator*, 31 January 1976)

The conclusion drawn from this hypothesis is that the full employment level of unemployment has risen substantially, and involuntary unemployment of the Keynesian type is not unduly high. As a result, the government is considered to be quite justified in raising its full employment target (in terms of unemployment) and to be concentrating on other economic problems such as inflation, industrial growth and the balance of payments.

When Keynes was writing during the depression of the 1930s he argued that the orthodox viewpoint of the day – the so-called classical theory which claimed that most unemployment was frictional or voluntary or was a result of excessive real wages – was not relevant to modern economic society. In the depression of the 1970s the adherents of the old classical school claim that Keynes is no longer relevant, if indeed he ever was.

In the following sections we shall carefully analyse the propositions of this 'new classical' theory. We begin by considering whether there is any evidence of a structural shift in the labour market. Although there is circumstantial evidence of a shift it does not go very far in explaining the very large increase in unemployment over the last decade. Furthermore, an examination of the specific effect of higher national insurance benefits and excessive wage claims on unemployment suggests that these factors are of minor significance. The implication is that we must look to other, involuntary, factors to explain the present high level of unemployment.

Structural changes in the labour market

There have been several attempts to classify the unemployment figures into demand-deficient and structural (including frictional) components. One estimation procedure, which involves calculating the amount of unregistered unemployment and the amount of labour which is 'hoarded' by firms during recessions, suggests that the upward trend in the rate of registered unemployed is almost entirely because of a trend increase in structural and institutional unemployment, from around zero in 1953–9 to about 2·3 per cent in 1973. (Worswick, 1976, p. 165)

An alternative approach was used by the National Institute of Economic and Social Research who compared unemployment rates with indicators of spare capacity at similar points in the trade cycle. (March 1966 and December 1973) Using these results in conjunction with other evidence, the National Institute argued that,

> Taken together, the evidence suggests that there has probably been a rather small increase in the full employment level of unemployment – an increase in the range of perhaps 100 – 200 thousand over the levels of the 1950s and early 1960s. This is not, from the point of view of macro-economic management, a major shift: if $1^1/_2$ per cent (about 350 thousand) represented full employment in the earlier period, then full employment in current circumstances might mean unemployment of 450–550 thousand (1·9 – 2·4 per cent). None of the evidence we have adduced can be used to justify a level significantly beyond this range. (NIESR, 1977, p. 51)

The above studies were carried out independently and used quite different methods to arrive at their results. Taken together they provide *prima facie* evidence of a structural change in the labour market. However, the implied full employment level of unemployment (about 500,000) is still well below the current level of unemployment and it still remains to be seen whether the structural change has been of a voluntary or involuntary nature. The key propositions of the 'new classical' theory, which argue that the increase has occurred voluntarily, are considered below.

National insurance benefits

One aspect of the 'new classical' thesis argues that welfare benefits had become so generous by the 1970s that many workers decided that it was no longer worth working for a living when a reasonable existence could be had on the dole. Even the unemployed who were actively looking for work could afford to look around a little longer before taking a new job. What evidence is there to support the view that high welfare benefits have actually induced more people to become unemployed and to remain unemployed for a longer time?

In this context, specific reference is often made to the impact of statutory redundancy payments and earnings-related supplements to unemployment benefit. In December 1965 the Redundancy Payments Act came into force. The Act provided a statutory right to redundancy payments for employees with a minimum of two years' continuous employment with their firm, the payments being related to weekly pay, age and length of service. In October 1966 the earnings-related supplement to unemployment benefit was introduced. The supplement is payable after two weeks' unemployment for a maximum period of six months.

It was thought that these benefits would enable people to stay on the unemployment register for longer periods of time, thus increasing the observed level of unemployment. If this theory is correct then two consequences might be expected to follow. First, there would be an increase in the number of registered unemployed for a given level of economic activity. Second, since vacancies would take, on average, longer to be filled, the level of vacancies would also rise. An early test of this theory was published by D. Gujarati in the *Economic Journal*. His analysis of the relationship between unemployment and vacancies revealed that the predicted consequences had occurred and that the significant turning point had been the end of 1966. (Gujarati, 1972) Indeed, a great deal of evidence is now available to show that after 1966 vacancies did not fall as much as expected on the basis of past relationships. Furthermore, vacancies rose much more rapidly than expected during 1972 and 1973. Does this provide, then, conclusive evidence that the 'full employment' level of unemployment has risen because of a voluntary increase in the duration of unemployment? In fact this evidence is inconclusive as it is consistent with quite a number of other theories. Even Gujarati admitted in a footnote that 'On grounds of logic and timing this legislation seems to be responsible for the upward trend in the registered unemployment rate observed since 1966 – IV (4th quarter). Of course, there may be other reasons which in conjunction with the Social Security legislation mentioned above may also explain the upward trend'. (*ibid.*, p. 202)

Many other hypotheses have been put forward which are consistent with the changed relationship of unemployment to vacancies after 1966. One argues that there has been an increase in the notification of vacancies because of the improved services offered by Department of Employment local offices. Another claims that because of a sudden 'shake out' of labour after 1966 employers became much more selective in choosing new workers and so took much longer to fill vacancies. In this way both unemployment and vacancies rose. In particular, it has been argued that the 1972/3 boom was so rapid that the available vacancies did not immediately match the skills and locations of the unemployed. As a result vacancies rose rapidly and unemployment did not fall as much as would normally be expected in a more leisurely reflation. It is clear then that all that has been proved is that there has been a change in the unemployment-vacancy relationship. What still requires proof is that it was the introduction of redundancy pay and earnings-related supplement that caused this change.

The direct evidence which is available on the effects of these benefits suggests, in fact, that they have had little effect on the duration, and hence the level, of unemployment. In chapter 3 we looked at the range of benefits available to the unemployed and we return here to the evidence particularly relevant to our argument. In the PEP study it was found that only 7 per cent of respondents had received payments under the Redundancy Payments Act. (Daniel, 1974, p. 117) The Department of Employment's own figures show that it is only a relatively small number of people that receive such payments. For instance, in the period January 1969 to May 1976 the average number of payments per month was approximately 21,000. This compares with an average inflow on to the unemployment register of about 330,000 per month over the same period. (DE, 1977, and *Unemployment Statistics*, 1972, Annex 2) The small numbers involved thus makes it highly unlikely that redundancy pay has had any substantial effect on unemployment. If all workers who received redundancy pay took two weeks longer to find a job than they would in the absence of the payment, unemployment would only be 10,000 higher than it would otherwise have been. (*ibid.*, p. 6) Even this appears to be rather on the high side if other evidence is considered. For instance, one study of redundant engineering workers found that once age and other factors had been taken into account the size of the redundancy payment did not appear to be significantly correlated with the length of time out of work. (Mackay and Reid, 1972) In addition, the OPCS study of the working of the Redundancy Payments Act found that 21 per cent of respondents started a new job in their next working day after being made redundant and a further 18 per cent started within two weeks. (Office of Population Censuses and Surveys, 1971)

We have already noted in Chapter 3 that the numbers claiming earnings-related supplement (ERS) are also relatively small. In this case, it has been estimated that the maximum possible effect on unemployment of the introduction of ERS was about 80,000. (*Unemployment Statistics*, 1972a, p. 10) If it were assumed that the receipt of the supplement doubled the length of an individual's spell of unemployment then the resultant increase in the level of unemployment would be about 50,000. (*ibid.*, p. 9) However, even this figure is likely to be an overestimate as the PEP study found that the majority of workers attached great importance to finding a job as soon as possible and that nearly 60 per cent started their job search immediately. (Daniel, 1974, pp. 122–3)

Excessive wage claims

The argument that excessively high wage claims during the 1970s have caused the current high level of unemployment is generally based on figures similar to those given in Table 8.1. These figures give an estimate for the last few years of the 'excess' real wage which is defined as the difference between the actual and the 'equilibrium' real wage. The latter is what is considered justified by movements in productivity and the terms of trade.

TABLE 8.1 *Actual and 'equilibrium' real earnings, 1973–6*

	(1) Index of real earnings*	(2) Terms of trade adjustment†	(3) Productivity adjustment	(4) 'Equilibrium' earnings	(5) % excess of real earnings
(*1973 I = 100*)					
1973 I	100·0	—	—	100·0	—
1974 I	96·9	−6·6	−2·7	90·7	6·8
1975 I	106·9	−6·1	−1·2	92·7	15·4
1976 I	104·5	−4·8	−1·4	93·8	11·5

* Seasonally adjusted index of average earnings divided by the retail price index (averages of three months).
† Based on unit value index for exports expressed as a percentage of the unit value index for imports.

NOTE: It is assumed that (i) average real earnings were at their equilibrium level during the first quarter of 1973; (ii) a 1 per cent change in the terms of trade requires 0·3 per cent change in the real wage as imports represent about 30 per cent of GDP; (iii) a 1 per cent change in productivity entails a 1 per cent change in real wages.
Equilibrium earnings in any quarter are therefore obtained by adding the terms of trade adjustment and the productivity adjustment to the real wage for the base period. Equilibrium earnings are then subtracted from actual real earnings and the difference expressed as a proportion of equilibrium earnings to give column (5). (For a further discussion of this concept see Hughes, 1976 and Flemming, 1976.)

(*Source: Economic Trends, 1977*)

Of course these figures merely illustrate an association between 'excess' real wages and unemployment – they imply nothing about causation. However, the theory is that if trade unions press for wages which are inconsistent with productivity and international competitiveness then firms will either suffer a profit squeeze or face greater international competition, with the result that workers will be laid off and unemployment will rise. If the government pursued reflationary policies this would merely cause an increase in prices and unions would only push up wages yet again.

The false option of big pay increases underwritten by government 'reflation' which merely means sufficient injections of new money to raise prices enough to cancel out the extra purchasing power of the nominally larger pay packets is easier to propound on political and trade union platforms. But there are increasingly encouraging signs that there is widespread recognition of the futility of that approach to unemployment. Trade unionists and others are coming more and more to see – as every greengrocer has always known – that there is only one reliable way to clear all your stock; and that is to charge a market-clearing price. (*The Times*, 13 December 1976)

The belief that excessively high wages cause unemployment is not at all new. It is the same theory that was used by the orthodox economists of the 1930s to support their claim that unemployment could only be cured by cuts in wages and that reflationary measures would not work. A prominent example of this point of view is that of A. C. Pigou who, in 1933, argued,

> With perfectly free competition ... there will always be at work a strong tendency for wage-rates to be so related to demand that everybody is employed .... The implication is that such unemployment as exists at any time is due wholly to the fact that changes in demand conditions are continually taking place and that frictional resistances prevent the appropriate wage adjustments from being made instantaneous. (Pigou, 1933, p. 252).

These 'frictional resistances' were of course the workers' resistance to wage cuts. 'If this broad conclusion is accepted it follows that long run government policies, which ... make the state of labour demand permanently better or worse than it would otherwise have been, are not, when once established, either causes of or remedies for unemployment'. (*ibid.*, p. 252)

In 1936 Keynes argued that the assumptions on which the classical theory was based were not applicable to the real world with the result that 'its teaching is misleading and disastrous if we attempt to apply it to the facts of experience'. (Keynes, 1936, p. 3). The key fallacy in the classical theory is the assumption that workers themselves have the power to determine the real wage and thus the ability (if not the will) to bring about a situation of full employment. As Keynes pointed out, this postulate:

> flows from the idea that the real wages of labour depend on the wage bargains which labour makes with the entrepreneurs. It is admitted, of course, that the bargains are actually made in terms of money, and even that the real wages acceptable to labour are not altogether

independent of what the corresponding money-wage happens to be. Nevertheless it is the money-wage thus arrived at which is held to determine the real wage. (*ibid.*, pp. 10–11).

Although this proposition may be true at the level of the individual firm it is clearly false if applied to the economy as a whole. For instance, if real wages are above their equilibrium level (that is, the level consistent with full employment) a reduction in average money wages (or more realistically a reduction in the rate of increase in money wages) would merely reduce effective demand, which in turn would tend to depress the level of prices (or their rate of increase). Real wages and unemployment would hardly be affected at all. As Keynes insisted, it is aggregate effective demand that determines employment and employment that determines the corresponding real wage – not the other way round.

Keynes's argument was intended to apply to the closed economy, that is, it ignored the effect of international trade. However, if international transactions are allowed for then the conclusion has to be slightly modified to admit that some unemployment may result from large increases in wage rates. One estimate suggests that if there is a once and for all 5 per cent increase in money wages then, assuming no other changes (including compensating action by the government and changes in the exchange rate), there will be a fall in unemployment of 0·2 percentage points within one year, but a rise of 0·2 percentage points within two years and of 0·5 percentage points within three years. (Pratten, 1972) The estimates are therefore quite small given the assumptions made. In practice, the effect of wage inflation will have been even smaller as wage inflation in other countries together with the substantial depreciation of the pound during the 1970s will have had significant compensatory effects. It is clear then that on the grounds of logic and empirical evidence the 'excessive' wage theory makes little contribution to explaining the high level of unemployment.

The above discussion has shown that there is little evidence to support the 'new classical' theory. Indeed, the findings of the PEP's unemployment survey suggest that, at a time when full employment had supposedly been reached, there existed only a very small element of voluntary unemployment.

The PEP survey showed that 73 per cent of their sample were concerned to find jobs but were unable to do so quickly. (Daniel, 1974, p. 27) This total excluded those who were not intending to work again, those attaching no importance to finding a job, and those finding a job within a month of losing the last. The figure would include structural as well as demand-deficient unemployment. It might also include a small number of people who although keen to work may be considered 'unemployable' because of disability or ill health.

The survey found that only 5 per cent of the unemployed could be considered as short-term or frictionally unemployed. This proportion represented people who had found a job within a month of losing the last. (*ibid.*, p. 25) If this percentage is applied to the total number of unemployed people at the time (about 500,000) then we arrive at an estimate of 25,000 as frictional unemployment. This is much lower than estimates quoted by the Centre for Policy Studies, who calculate this type of unemployment by taking the number of people registered as unemployed for four weeks or less. Chapter 1 has detailed the fallacious nature of the Centre for Policy Studies' argument which ignores the fact that many of those who, at a particular time, have been unemployed for less than a month may well remain on the register for a much longer time. (For evidence on this point see DE, 1974a, p. 180.)

We noted in Chapter 1 that 22 per cent of the PEP respondents said that they had no intention of finding a job or attached little importance to doing so. Furthermore, we also pointed out that this number (about 110,000 if the percentage is applied to total unemployment at that time) contained many who were sick, injured or disabled (about 3·6 per cent or 18,000), those who were nearing retirement age and women who were not in a position to work for family or domestic reasons. It may also have included people who, because of a feeling of being rejected by society, gave the impression of being rather carefree about their situation. There was little evidence of any large-scale voluntary unemployment in the sense of people registering as unemployed but who were fit and able to work. At first, this appears to be in conflict with other evidence. For instance, reference is often made to 50,000 occupational pensioners who register as unemployed but only do so in order to qualify for national insurance benefits (these rules have recently been changed). (Wood, 1975, p. 21) The idea is given that the pensioners are not seeking work since their occupational pension effectively means that they can enjoy an early retirement. However, as we have seen in Chapter 1, a more careful consideration of the evidence paints quite a different picture. The evidence is a survey undertaken by the Department of Employment in June 1973 of the characteristics of the unemployed. For the occupational pensioners it was found that only a third of them had pensions of more than £20 per week, and that a quarter were receiving less than £5. (DE 1974a, p. 220) To argue that these pensioners are all voluntarily unemployed is clearly not consistent with the facts.

In any case the existence of voluntary unemployment begs the question of cause and effect. The observation of men who do not appear to be very enthusiastic about looking for work does not necessarily prove that it is their indifferent and workshy attitude that has caused their unemployment. It could equally be argued that it has been a long period of unemployment that has caused this attitude. This was recognised even in the 1930s as the following extract from an Unemployment Assistance Board report shows:

> Of greater dimensions, and in some respects of greater difficulty, is the problem that arises in the case of applicants who would probably accept work if it were offered to them but have fallen into such a condition of mind and body that they make no personal effort to obtain it. Neither is it likely in view of their lack of skill and loss of industrial efficiency that, in the normal course, an offer of employment would be made to them. These men are usually the victims of their own prolonged unemployment, which has produced a state of indifference and lassitude that tends to become progressively worse .... Many of these men who have thus drifted into the backwaters of industrial life are potentially good and efficient workers, but the immediate necessity is to restore in them that physical condition and that habit of work without which they are unlikely to keep any reasonably paid and regular employment. (Unemployment Assistance Board, 1938, p. 5)

This extract clearly identifies one of the basic problems of distinguishing between voluntary and involuntary unemployment. For the suggestion being made is that long periods of involuntary unemployment may in fact affect people's attitude to work such that they appear to be voluntarily unemployed. A further point to be considered is that although people may originally become voluntarily unemployed in the confident expectation of finding another job, they may, after a period of time, find that their expectations are not realised and consequently become involuntarily unemployed.

Involuntary structural unemployment

In contrast to the 'new classical' theory, it has been suggested that the increase in unemployment is due to structural factors of an involuntary nature. For instance, Jim Taylor has argued that the post-1966 upward shift in unemployment reflects a once-and-for-all 'shake out' of 'hoarded' labour. Previously, labour had been hoarded by firms during short-run downturns in demand and output in order to retain an experienced and trained work force so that, when demand and output revived, suitable labour would be readily available. However, the introduction of Selective Employment Tax, productivity bargaining, the increase in merger activity and the growing emphasis during the 1960s on rationalisation and efficiency led firms to reduce the amount of hoarded labour. Although Taylor has put forward some evidence of de-hoarding the results have been questioned and other statistical tests provide little support for the 'shake-out' hypothesis. (Taylor, 1972)

TABLE 8.2: *Percentage share of plant and machinery in gross fixed investment, United Kingdom 1963–76*

		% of total gross fixed capital formation*		
	Years of cyclically low unemployment	%	Years of cyclically high unemployment	%
Manufacturing industry	1961	71·1	1963	72·4
	1965	71·8	1968	76·0
	1969	74·5	1972	75·3
	1974	75·3	1976†	77·2
Total economy	1962**	37·5	1963	38·6
	1965	38·1	1968	36·7
	1969	37·6	1972	34·9
	1974	38·5	1976†	36·1

* At 1970 prices
† First three quarters only
** A comparable figure for 1961 is not available

(*Sources: Economic Trends annual supplement,* 1976; *Economic Trends,* 1977)

Another theory is that the full employment level of unemployment has increased because of a rapid change in the economy's employment structure. Particular reference is made to the rapid fall in manufacturing employment during the past fifteen years; nearly $1\frac{1}{2}$ million jobs have been lost in manufacturing industry over the last decade. A change of such large proportions is certain to have put a significant strain on the economy's ability to provide new jobs outside the manufacturing sector.

A contributory factor to this shedding of labour is the increased capital-intensity of manufacturing investment. Although direct quantitative measures are not available, circumstantial evidence of this process is given in Table 8.2. These figures compare the percentages of fixed investment represented by plant and machinery in both manufacturing industry and in the whole economy. An increased proportion of capital expenditure taken up by plant and machinery is an indirect indicator of more capital-intensive methods as labour-intensive methods would be expected to generate expenditure on other forms of fixed investment, such as vehicles and new buildings. As the table shows there has been an upward trend in the proportion of manufacturing investment represented by plant and machinery with particularly large increases in the 1965–8 and the 1974–6 recessions. Taking the economy as a whole, though, there does not appear to have been an overall upward trend.

The effect of the loss in manufactuirng jobs on unemployment has been compounded by the recent increase in the working population. For example, total civilian employees (both employed and unemployed) fell from 23·0 million in mid-1966 to 22·8 million in mid-1971. However, by the middle of 1976 the total has increased by one million (an average yearly increase of 200,000). (DE, 1974a; 1977) The figures relate to Great Britain. As we point out below, this increase is largely explained by an increase in the teenage population and in female economic activity.

We noted in Chapter 2 several distinguishing aspects of unemployment in the present recession. Two of these features, illustrated in Table 8.3, are the increased unemployment among school leavers and among women. These changes are particularly relevant to this discussion and can be partially explained by demographic changes, amounting to a structural change in the composition of the labour force.

TABLE 8.3 *Unemployment in Great Britain* * *1969–76*

June of each year	Non-school leavers (000)		School leavers (000)	Total (000)
	Males	Females		
1969	413·3	67·7	2·3	483·3
1970	448·5	72·6	2·6	523·6
1971	585·7	96·6	4·9	687·2
1972	641·0	116·0	8·4	765·5
1973	458·6	82·7	3·6	545·0
1974	435·8	73·4	5·4	514·6
1975	668·4	141·8	18·4	828·5
1976	906·0	253·7	118·2	1277·9

* Excluding adult students and unadjusted for seasonal variations

(*Source*: DE, 1977; British Labour Statistics Yearbooks, 1969 to 1972)

First, if we consider the period 1965 onwards, there was a steady fall in the youth population (that is, persons aged 15–19 inclusive) from 4·1 million in 1965 to 3·7 million in 1970. Since that time there has been a steady rise in the number of youths, with an increase of 2·4 per cent in 1975 and a projected increase of 2·7 per cent in 1976 and 2·5 per cent in 1977. The direct effect of this demographic change has been to increase the number of school leavers by almost 100,000 (14 per cent) between the school years 1969–70 and 1975–6. (Dean, 1976) All the figures quoted relate to Great Britain.

Second, there has been a marked increase in the number of women passing through the employment offices which, together with the rise in female employees, points to an increase in female economic activity. Between 1967 and 1974 the number of females joining or leaving the unemployment register remained fairly constant even during the course of successive trade cycles. However, during 1975 there was a marked change in the size of the flows which continued into 1976. A change of similar proportions did not occur for men. This phenomenon cannot be explained by an increase in the female population of working age (that is, 15–59 inclusive). Although there was a small increase in 1976 and a slightly larger projected increase in 1976, it is almost entirely accounted for by an increase in the 15–19 age group, a problem which has been discussed above. (See *Population Trends 6*, Winter 1976, DE, 1977 and OPCS, 1976) The increase in female economic activity may not be a purely structural change in the sense of being totally independent of demand. Indeed it illustrates how structural unemployment is dependent to some degree on demand for the rise in the number of women looking for jobs must partly be a symptom of the depth of the current depression which has forced wives and mothers into the labour market to try and supplement the family income.

The above factors go some way towards explaining the recent structural shift in the labour market. However, in spite of the existence of these changes, we have yet to explain why the current level of unemployment is so much higher than the full employment level which independent estimates suggest to be in the region of 500,000. The discussion now turns to the effect of changes in aggregate demand on the level of unemployment. We shall show that this is a significant factor in explaining the recent unprecedented levels of unemployment, implying that there is a large amount of involuntary unemployment which could be reduced to the benefit of society.

Demand-deficient unemployment

Figure 8.2 compares movements in the unemployment rate with changes in aggregate demand (measured by changes in the growth rate of real gross domestic product). It clearly shows that the dramatic change in unemployment levels since 1966 is largely explained by an unprecedented drop in aggregate demand. The relationship is closest in the periods 1960–5 and 1972–6. In 1966 a large increase in unemployment occurred when at the same time demand remained fairly constant. However, this change may have partly been a lagged response to the severe drop in demand between 1964 and 1965. The relationship is far less close between 1969 and 1972.

Table 8.4 shows recent changes in the individual components of aggregate demand. The current depression has been marked by a sharp drop not only in consumers' expenditure, by far the largest component of aggregate demand, but also in exports and particularly in private investment.

TABLE 8.4 *Changes in components of aggregate demand* 1971–6*

Percentage change in constant 1970 prices

	Consumers' expenditure	Public authorities' consumption	Private fixed investment	Public fixed investment	Exports
1971	+ 2·7	+ 2·7	+ 4·7	−0·6	+ 7·2
1972	+ 5·8	+ 4·1	+ 5·7	−3·2	+ 2·2
1973	+ 4·5	+ 4·2	+ 5·2	+ 2·6	+ 11·9
1974	−0·9	+ 1·9	−4·6	+ 2·3	+ 7·1
1975	−0·7	+ 4·7	−2·8	+ 1·1	−3·8
1976†	0·0	+ 3·5	−6·5	−1·0	+ 5·4

* The percentage shares of these components of total final expenditure on goods and services at market prices for the first three quarters of 1976 are as follows (per cent): consumers' expenditure 50·0; public authorities' consumption 15·6; private fixed investment 7·7; public fixed investment 5·8; exports 21·1.
† First three quarters only (seasonally adjusted).

(*Source*: *Economic Trends*, 1977)

The impact of demand on unemployment has also been noted by the National Institute of Economic and Social Research. In December 1976 the National Institute conducted a survey of both large and small companies accounting for some 15 per cent of manufacturing employment. The results of the questionnaire suggested that, *if demand existed*,

> it would be possible with existing capital capacity to increase output in manufacturing industry by some $7\frac{1}{2}$ per cent with the existing labour force and hours of work, by about $12\frac{1}{2}$ per cent with the same labour force but longer hours of work, and by over 20 per cent if labour were readily available. (NIESR, 1977, p. 47)

Furthermore, by constructing certain statistical measures of capacity (utilisation, the existence of a very large degree of spare capacity) in manufacturing was pointed to (about 7 to 14 per cent depending on the particular assumptions made about the growth of capacity since the previous peak output year). The National Institute concluded that,

> The evidence is that there is a quite unprecedented degree of unemployment of resources – both labour and capital – in the British economy. Gross domestic product is probably nearly 10 per cent below the full employment level, and the evidence from both our panel enquiry and from the statistical measurement of capacity utilisation is

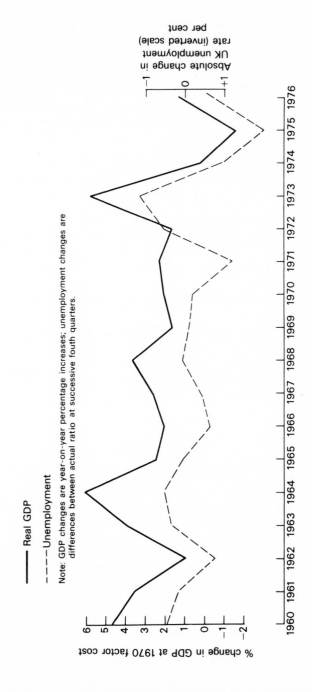

FIGURE 8.2 Unemployment and aggregate demand, UK, 1960–76
(*Source: Economic Trends, Annual supplement 1976, Economic Trends 1977, DE, 1977*)

that the increased output needed to return to full employment could be produced with existing capital capacity and with only isolated occurrences of shortages of skilled labour. All that is lacking is demand, but the long-standing problem of how to stimulate demand through investment and exports, rather than through consumption, remains. (*ibid.*; p. 51)

Conclusion

We have argued in this chapter that the unprecedented rise in unemployment is largely explained by a deficiency in aggregate demand. We have also found evidence of a structural shift in the labour market which has raised the full employment level of unemployment to something in the order of 500,000. Several explanations of this shift have been discussed but we have firmly rejected the 'new classical' theory which invokes high national insurance benefits and excessive wage claims as the prime causes of unemployment. The implication of this theory is that, as the increase in unemployment has been largely voluntary, then the 'socially acceptable' rate of unemployment has substantially increased and that the government can reasonably turn its attention to other, more important, policy problems. This conclusion has been found to be entirely unwarranted by the available evidence. Indeed in the light of so much evidence it seems strange that these views have become so entrenched in orthodox circles. A similar situation existed in the 1930s when the orthodox classical economists were still arguing that mass unemployment was largely voluntary. As Keynes pointed out,

> The classical theorists resemble Euclidean geometers in a non-Euclidean world who, discovering that in experience straight lines apparently parallel often meet, rebuke the lines for not keeping straight – as the only remedy for the unfortunate collisions which are occurring. Yet, in truth, there is no remedy except to throw over the axiom of parallels and to work out a non-Euclidean geometry. (Keynes, 1936, p. 16)

A similar overthrow of the classical paradigm is required today.

9 Government action against unemployment

Frank Field and Stephen Winyard

Introduction

It is widely recognised that unemployment can only effectively be tackled by national economic policies. However, in the past three years the government has taken a number of short-term measures to try to reduce the numbers out of work. Many of these measures have been aimed at young workers and the Minister has argued that they are 'unprecedented in their nature and scale, and in our view they amount to a formidable battery of weapons with which to fight the scourge of unemployment.' (*Hansard*, 1976f, col. 1118) In this chapter we examine these weapons to maintain and create jobs, as well as the training and retraining programmes that have been expanded by the government in an attempt to improve and extend the skills of the unemployed and thus help them to find work. Most of the chapter is concerned with describing the series of measures which make up the programme, the amounts of money committed to the various schemes, and the number of jobs involved. We conclude with an assessment of these special measures in tackling Britain's growing unemployment problem. But we first need to say a word about the Manpower Services Commission (MSC) through which the programme is administered. The MSC began operating in 1974 and has the responsibility for the great majority of the unemployment services. It operates through two agencies: the Employment Services Agency (ESA) and the Training Services Agency (TSA). The ESA has control over the public employment service. The TSA is responsible for all aspects of training, including the Training Opportunities Scheme (TOPS), co-ordinating the work of the Industrial Training Boards, and running the skillcentres.

What measures have been taken since 1974 to alleviate unemployment? In this chapter we are focusing on the creation and maintenance of jobs, the training and retraining of workers, and policies to help workers move on to jobs from areas of high unemployment. The first approach attempts to tackle unemployment directly by providing more jobs or by protecting jobs that are threatened. The second approach is indirect and will only be successful if workers are provided with appropriate training; that is if training is closely related to the job vacancies existing in an area. If the vacancies are not available then this approach merely produces a more highly skilled pool of unemployed. The third approach, encouraging workers to move to a different part of the country to find work, is similar to the second in that it does not involve increasing the total number of jobs in the economy. Again it aims purely at a better match, in this case geographically, between vacancies and the unemployed.

The Job Creation Programme

The Job Creation Programme (JCP) was announced by the government in September 1975 and launched by the MSC in October. Based on a Canadian model of work creation, it has been described by the Secretary of State as 'an essential emergency response' to high unemployment, particularly amongst young workers. (*Hansard*, 1976f, col. 1123) The aim of the JCP is to provide 'worthwhile jobs' for people who would otherwise be unemployed with particular emphasis being given to the 16–24 and 50–plus age groups. A number of additional criteria have been laid down which must be met if a project is to receive JCP money; in particular that the work should benefit the local community, either through the improvement of the local environment or by assisting in the solution of social or community problems. JCP grants are meant to cover the wages and national insurance contributions of workers with a discretionary addition (up to 10 per cent of the total wages bill) to cover administration and capital expenses.

Approximately two-thirds of the 4,600 projects agreed to the end of 1976 have been sponsored by local authorities and other statutory authorities. The remainder have been set up by voluntary and charitable organisations, community groups, trade unions, youth organisations and the like. A few examples from a recent analysis of the JCP indicate the range of projects and sponsors (Table 9.1).

It is intended that projects established with JCP money should be of a short-term nature, twelve months is the maximum period for funding. However eight projects have been set up on the basis that they aim for long-term viability. But as a junior Minister at the Department of Employment recently observed, 'It is too early to say how many will achieve this aim.' (*Hansard*, 1976m, col. 711)

£30m was allocated to the JCP when it was introduced in the autumn of 1975, with a further £10m in December. In February 1976 the programme was reviewed and an extra £30m allocated to keep the scheme going until the end of the year. However a further re-assessment took place in the late spring and it was decided to put an extra £20m into

TABLE 9.1 *Range of sponsors and job opportunities under the job creation programme*

Sponsor	Project
Teesside Industrial Mission	A workshop employing forty-four disabled or educationally subnormal young people. The work includes re-furbishing of school and church furniture and the manufacture of wooden toys and play equipment.
Newport Women's Aid	Five people helping with the administrative work of the refuge and with care of children, organising play groups, etc.
General and Municipal Workers Union	Thirteen people building a centre for handicapped children.
Liverpool Sailing Club	Twenty-eight people working on the extension of existing club buildings to provide storage for club rescue boats and a lookout control tower.

the programme to secure its work until September 1977.

Initially it was decided that the JCP should apply only to the Assisted Areas. The government did, however, respond to pressures from other parts of the country with high unemployment and make the programme generally available. The regional distribution of JCP money allocated up to the beginning of November 1976 is set out in Table 9.2.

TABLE 9.2 *Regional allocation of JCP money*

Area	Allocation (£m)	No. of jobs approved up to 5 November 1976
Scotland	21·0	13,700
Wales	9·5	5,200
London and South-East	5·0	2,500
Northern	14·0	8,100
South-West	4·5	3,200
Yorkshire and Humberside	6·0	3,400
Midlands	4·5	3,300
North-West	7·0	4,000
Merseyside	13·0	6,300

(*Source*: DE, 1976f)

What has the JCP achieved? Looking firstly at the number of jobs created we can see from Table 9.2 that by the beginning of November, thirteen months after the start of the programme, a little under 50,000 jobs had been created. The aim of the government is for the programme to create approximately 90,000 jobs over the twenty-four months up to September 1977. However, this figure can be misleading. It should be noted that the average length of projects is thirty-one weeks. One in eight projects last less than twelve weeks. Therefore at any one time the number of people at work because of the scheme is quite small. For example on 30 January 1977 there were 620 approved projects offering job opportunities to 7,949 persons. Yet even this total overestimates the number of employment opportunities. Of the 620 approved projects only 242 had commenced. (*Hansard*, 1976a, col. 582) For some people the programme is just a short interlude of work within a much longer period of unemployment.

A second aim of the JCP is that projects should benefit both the local community in which they are carried out, and the people employed. An examination of the type of projects funded under the programme indicates that the first part of this objective has in general been satisfied. Indeed the programme seems to have cast its net very widely and taken in projects that under more tightly defined criteria might have been excluded. However some people have argued that the programme has not cast its net widely enough. A major criticism of the JCP from the Conservative Party has been that 'the private sector has not been allowed to take on people under the programme where there was any opportunity of making a profit.' (*Hansard*, 1976f, col. 1112) The Shadow Employment Secretary argued for a much greater role for private industry in the scheme.

The difficulties faced by the private sector in participating in the scheme were highlighted in evidence by the MSC to the Social Services and Employment Sub-Committee of the House of Commons Expenditure Committee. In the three months to February 1977 only 4 per cent of job projects were in the private sector, compared to 2 per cent in the first year of the programme. The main reason for this, according to the MSC evidence, was that 'most employers have found it difficult to find projects which adhere to the criteria of having community benefit and which would not yield any profit.' (*Financial Times*, 10 February 1977)

Regarding the benefit of JCP schemes to the people employed on them the achievements are far more patchy. Many of the projects, and particularly those included in the largest category which is 'Improvement of land, parks and forests', have almost no training element. Employed on unskilled work, the young people recognise that there's little or no point to it. Cleaning slogans from walls and knocking down war-time defences leads to disillusionment and clearly doesn't prepare people for a career.

Towards the end of 1976 whilst interviewing in Liverpool members of the Low Pay Unit visited two JCPs set up by the Rathbone Society. They contrasted strongly and help to illustrate the strengths of programmes with a major training element, and the weaknesses of some environmental projects. One project employed six youths between the ages of 16 and 20 on 'environmental work'; a number of derelict sites in Liverpool 8 were being turned into gardens and play areas. The other project had involved setting up a workshop to make a wide range of products in wood for local schools, playgroups, and residents. Four skilled craftsmen are employed at the workshop and they are training ten youths.

The workshop has been very successful. A large number of orders are being received, two local firms have made donations allowing machinery to be purchased, and the trainees are being prepared for a career in carpentry. Day release to the local Technical College provides formal training in addition to the practical guidance provided by the craftsmen. The trainees saw themselves as very lucky at having been selected for the workshop. 'It's great, I'm learning a skill,' and 'I'll be all right for a job now,' were the sort of views expressed. For those employed on the environmental project the JCP looked rather different. Grateful to have a job they were, however, acutely aware that it wasn't leading anywhere.

Another obvious benefit of the JCP to the people employed on projects is the wages they receive. JCP grants are designed to cover the wages of projects, wages being set at the 'going rate' for the type of job created. In Liverpool the going rate for young workers was very low, and the projects paid £18 per week at 16, £21 at 17, and £24 for workers aged 18 and over. However the craftsmen received more than this; much closer to the JCP upper limit of £56 per week. In the House of Commons the Shadow Employment Secretary criticised the JCP on a number of occasions for paying wages of £56. 'That is an unnecessary waste of Government money and it means that a lot of money is being spent on only a few people.' (*Hansard*, 1976f, col. 1112)

Temporary Employment Subsidy

The Temporary Employment Subsidy scheme (TES) was introduced in August 1975. The main aim of the scheme is to persuade firms to defer planned redundancies, and the Secretary of State when announcing it said,

> It is my earnest hope that this scheme will contribute significantly to limiting additions to unemployment in the particularly hard hit areas by helping employers to get over temporary difficulties and maintain their labour force and by enabling work people either to avoid the upheaval of redundancy or to gain time for retraining or re-deployment. (DE, 1976b, p. 464)

Initially the scheme applied only to companies in the Assisted Areas which were planning '50 or more' redundancies. However in September 1975 it was extended to the whole country. In addition the level of qualifying redundancy has been reduced in stages: by February 1976 firms considering laying off '10 or more' workers became eligible. A number of conditions must be met for firms to qualify for a subsidy:

(a) They must not be insolvent or about to become insolvent,
(b) the Department of Employment must have been notified of the impending redundancies in accordance with the provisions of the Employment Protection Act,
(c) consultations should have begun with the trade unions concerned and the application must be made jointly with the application form being signed by both the company and the trade unions,
(d) the current pay limit must not be exceeded.

The subsidy is paid to the company and was originally set at £10 per week for each prospectively redundant full-time worker. The maximum period for payments to a firm was set at six months but in February 1976 this was extended. Payments are now reviewed after three months and if the conditions are still satisfied can run for another nine months. In the April 1976 Budget the payment was raised to £20 per worker.

It was made clear when the scheme was introduced that it was an experiment. As we have seen, the government must view it as something of a success in that the eligibility criteria have been progressively widened and the level of payment per worker raised. The life of the scheme has also been extended. It was originally to run for a period of twelve months, but in April 1976 it was announced that applications could be made up to the end of 1976. A further extension was announced in the December 'mini-budget', applications are being received up to 30 April 1977. By January 1977, 2565 applications had been approved since the inception of the scheme and 184,834 jobs preserved at a gross cost of £175m. (*Hansard*, 1977d, col. 548) This expenditure has, not surprisingly, been concentrated in a few industries, in particular clothing and textiles. (*Hansard*, 1977c, cols. 449–50)

Undoubtedly the TES scheme has been successful in preserving a considerable number of jobs. However, it should be remembered that the subsidy is a temporary one, at a maximum it can be paid for twelve months. What happens to jobs when the subsidy ceases? Certainly some applications have been successful. An article on the scheme published in the May 1976 *Gazette* gave a number of case histories of firms that had applied for a subsidy and thus avoided redundancies. One knitwear firm had used the time gained through a TES to retrain 50 women workers so that they could move into the more profitable leisurewear division. A large textile company was about to make 400 workers redundant because of a shortage of work. It applied for a subsidy and within six months improved orders and some retraining had removed the threat of redundancy.

In these two cases the TES has allowed the firm to get over temporary difficulties. However, the final outcome for some of the other firms receiving TES grants reported in the article is much less certain. One subsidy is, for example, giving a 'temporary reprieve ... in the hope that the firm would become more profitable'. In another case the subsidy is 'to provide a skilled work force against a future upturn in trade'. For a third firm it is 'enabling the company to maintain the labour force intact in readiness for an anticipated improvement in orders during 1976.' It appears that the scheme is particularly attractive to companies contemplating laying off skilled workers who, nevertheless, believe trade may soon begin to pick up. The retained skilled labour force would allow such companies to get back onto full production much more quickly than if they had to start recruiting a new work force. For example, one paper mill spokesman is reported as saying it was only worthwhile claiming the subsidy (which might involve dipping into reserves to meet the wages bill for subsidised workers) 'because we have to recruit and train our own labour'. The 180,000 or so jobs which have been protected, albeit perhaps temporarily, because of the TES have led one Department of Employment spokesman to say that it has been 'undoubtedly one of the most successful of recent schemes introduced to alleviate unemployment.' (*Financial Times*, 17 November 1976)

The work experience programme

One initiative which is proving to be less than successful is the work experience programme. In September 1976 the MSC approved the first batch of plans which it hoped would ultimately give 30,000 young people a minimum six months of working life in factories, offices or shops. The scheme was designed to help some of the 100,000 young people who the MSC estimated would be unemployed by the end of that year. Recruits are paid a government allowance of £16 a week tax free. The government expects the savings on unemployment and supplementary benefits to equal about half the £90m gross cost of the scheme.

In early January 1977 press reports began to appear on the scaling down of the scheme; because it was failing to get the support from industry which the government expected, the provisional places for youngsters were cut to 20,000. By Christmas 1976, the half-way mark for the scheme, the total number of places available was just over 6,000. These had been provided under 744 local schemes. Another hundred or so were waiting approval while a handful had been turned down because arrangements did not come up to the standards laid down by the MSC.

However, Parliamentary Answers given during the early months of 1977 paint an even more gloomy picture of the number of young persons in post. By 5 January 1977 only 4,623 young people had been recruited under the provisions of the work experience programme. (*Hansard*, 1977f, col. 87)

One reason why the scheme has not lived up to initial expectations is the relatively poor response from big companies. While a considerable number of them have joined in the scheme, the TSA maintains that, on the whole, they are not providing as many places per company as their size and importance as employers would warrant. Of those places available a high proportion are in commerce rather than manufacturing. A senior official of the TSA has been reported as saying

> it is not necessarily a question of manufacturing employers being less willing to cooperate. Many of them are having difficulty getting union agreement at plant level, despite the TUC's backing for the principle, and in some cases they are up against the factory's safety rules. (*TES*, 1 January 1977)

Community industry

The community industry scheme was started by the Conservative Government in 1972. It is included in our consideration of present job creation schemes because of its obvious relevance, and because of the expansion of places since 1974. Community industry projects are aimed at helping young people who have found particular difficulty in 'settling into stable jobs'. The hope is that by supervising these young people while they are undertaking practical projects, the scheme will be preparing them for regular employment in as short a time as possible. Each project consists of up to ten young workers and is usually supervised by skilled workers. Examples of projects include decorating and renovating, and the construction of adventure playgrounds.

Originally the scheme was designed to secure 2,000 jobs, but this was expanded to 3,000 places in August 1975 and to 4,000 by the end of 1975. In the April 1976 budget it was announced that the last 1,000 places would continue beyond March 1977 if the need for them still existed. At the same time the scheme was put on the same footing as the JCP in that approved projects were allowed a materials grant of up to 10 per cent of the labour costs. So far 8,500 young people have been given job opportunities under the scheme and by the end of 1976 approximately half this number found full-time employment after completing their time with a project. (NCSS, 1977) The cost of the scheme for 1976/7 has been put at £5·5m and will rise to just over £7m in a full year. The European Social Fund has contributed sizeable sums towards the cost of the project, for example, £1m in 1975.

Youth Employment Subsidy

From 13 October 1975 employers were paid £5 for twenty-six weeks for each unemployed school leaver employed who had not had a previous job. This initial stage of the scheme was called the recruitment subsidy for school leavers. The jobs provided have to be full time or for a fixed period of short duration. The scheme was extended in February 1976 to cover those who had left school in the summer of 1975. By the end of August 1976 29,574 school leavers had found jobs with the help of the subsidy. About a quarter of these were in the distributive trades and half in other service industries.

The recruitment subsidy for school leavers was expected to help about 30,000 young people at a cost of £3m. On 1 October 1976 it was replaced by the Youth Employment Subsidy scheme under which employers in the public or private sectors are paid £10 a week for up to twenty-six weeks for recruiting any person under 20 who has been unemployed for six months. The scheme, which is estimated to cost £5·4m, will run to the end of March 1978 and, like its predecessor, it is expected to provide help to 30,000 unemployed young people. By insisting that the subsidy will only be paid to young workers who have previously been unemployed for six months the government claims that it will provide 'more effective assistance where it is needed most: its aim is to help all long term unemployed young people.' (Treasury, 1976a)

Job-release scheme

This attempt to reduce the numbers of unemployed came into operation on 3 January 1977. The job release scheme only operates in Assisted Areas and caters for two main groups. The first consists of those men and women who are within one year of normal retiring age in the six-month period ending 30 June 1977. The scheme offers them the chance of retiring a year early. This has to be agreed by the worker with his employer who, in turn, has to undertake to recruit someone from the unemployment register to fill a full-time job, although it need not necessarily be the job from which a person is seeking early retirement. The allowance amounts to £23 a week, tax free.

The second group covered by the scheme are those registered unemployed who are within one year of reaching retirement. Early returns on the scheme show that by 28 January 1977, 5,178 applications had been approved under the job release scheme and of these 75 per cent were people already unemployed. The gross cost of the scheme which is to run for six months, is put at about £70m. The net cost when account is taken of savings of unemployment benefit is about £27m. (*Hansard*, 1976n, col. 92). Over half the approved applications have been granted to persons living in the North-West and in Yorkshire and Humberside. (*Financial Times*, 4 February 1977)

In its initial statement on the job release scheme it was made clear that the government hoped to encourage a considerable number of older workers to retire early and make a job available to a younger person. Yet any married man aged 64 earning £26·60 a week gross, assuming he has no dependant children or mortgage repayments, and any single person earning more than £38·60 a week, will be taking home more than the £23 a week job-release grant. It is therefore likely that most of the applications for the grant will not only come from unemployed persons, but will be concentrated amongst unemployed married men who are ineligible for the full earnings-related national insurance benefit and single unemployed persons. The advantage to the government of applicants from the ranks of the unemployed is that, once they are drawing the new grant, they are no longer counted in the total of unemployed.

Training and mobility

Earlier we outlined other ways by which the government can reduce the level of unemployment. One of these was to initiate training schemes so that workers can acquire a new range of skills, while the other means of reducing unemployment was by the provision of mobility grants so as to ease the migration of workers from areas of very high unemployment to those parts of the country where it is easier to obtain work. The assumption behind both these approaches is that, on the one hand, there is a serious mismatch between the skills needed by employers and those that workers are able to offer, and that a range of job opportunities exist in some areas of the country where there are shortages of applicants. We now turn to consider the range of training provisions and mobility allowances.

The main thrust of the government's training programme is divided between the Training Opportunities Scheme (TOPS) which is the responsibility of the TSA, and the Industrial Training Boards (ITBs). TOPS was initiated in 1972 in order to meet the requirements for training of individuals who had failed to acquire such skills when they were at school, or whose skills had become outdated, or were not of high enough level to seize promotion opportunities. TOPS offers 8,000 training courses. The great majority are either offered in the TSA's own skillcentres, of which there are sixty, or in Colleges of Further

Education. A minority of these courses are conducted in firms or private colleges. Courses at the skillcentres are overwhelmingly concerned with manual trades skills and those at colleges focus on commercial and clerical skills.

The Training Services Agency also works closely with the twenty-four Industrial Training Boards. Set up under the 1964 Industrial Training Act the Boards attempt to improve the scope and quality of training in their particular industries. The Employment and Training Act 1973 allows firms to gain exemption from the training levy, provided that their own training courses meet the ITB's requirements. This industrial training levy helps to spread the cost of training across the whole industry. Schemes to provide direct assistance to industry with its training costs are worked out between the TSA and the Boards. Such direct assistance is the other main way in which the TSA is attempting to maintain the level of training in a period of high unemployment. Particular emphasis is put on apprenticeships and the Chancellor of the Exchequer in early 1976 argued that 'we must do everything possible to build up scarce skills which will be in demand when the economy is running nearer to full employment.' (*Hansard*, 1976b, col. 637) In its first five-year plan, the TSA highlighted the effects on training of running the economy at a high level of unemployment. This was followed by a detailed study of the likely needs in the training field if unemployment continued to rise. On the basis of this study the Commission was able to submit contingency plans to the government in early 1975. From that date the government has given the MSC a total of £143m for counter-cyclical training measures.

Despite these initiatives, training schemes have still only a limited scope in this country. The MSC's chairman, Sir Denis Barnes, has drawn attention to the fact that in Britain about three-fifths of young people entering employment for the first time each year go into jobs where they receive no training or no training of real value. Sir Denis has argued that our training record compares badly with that of our partners in the EEC. For example, in Germany the equivalent of an apprenticeship system covers almost four-fifths of the jobs entered by young people. In Sweden seven out of every ten young people not going into higher education are undergoing vocational education courses lasting at least three years.

Nevertheless, we should note the increased emphasis on the provision of relevant training for the labour force. This has been one of the more optimistic developments over the past five years. In 1972 29,000 persons were trained by the Department of Employment. By 1976 the TSA was training almost 90,000; in the region of 10,000 above the planned number. Moreover, a considerable number of those who have completed their training courses return to full-time employment. Although the position has deteriorated since 1972 when eight out of every ten trainees entered full-time employment or further training, some 69 per cent of trainees in 1975 got a full-time job after completing their course. (*Hansard*, 1977f, col. 82)

Job search

The job-search scheme was initiated on 5 November 1975 with the aim of helping unemployed people look for work outside their own neighbourhoods. Help is given with fares and living expenses to those who are attempting to seek a job outside their local labour market. Candidates are allowed to claim interview expenses for jobs they are seeking. The claimants are required to furnish evidence from the prospective employer that they not only have an interview, but a reasonable chance of winning the job. Those living outside the Assisted Areas must also be able to show that there is no reasonable prospect of suitable employment within easy distance of the claimant's home. The only figures available on the number of persons assisted under this scheme is 10,160 for the period 1 January to 30 September 1976. (*Hansard*, 1977, col. 676)

Employment transfer scheme

This scheme is run by the Employment Services Agency and is mainly aimed to help people living in the Assisted Areas. It provides a system of grants and allowances to redundant and unemployed people of all ages to find new jobs in other areas. The applicant must first find a new job and within six months notify the local job centre or employment office of his intention of seeking help under this scheme. Transferred workers are able to claim free fares to take up work or visit a spouse or dependant, a settling-in grant to cover immediate expenses when starting work and a temporary separation allowance for any week during which three days are spent in lodgings away from a spouse or dependants. This temporary separation allowance can be drawn for up to two years from the date of starting work. In addition, an allowance to cover fares for visits home may be claimed up to twelve times in any one year.

If the transferred worker still has housing costs or storage charges to meet, a continuing liability allowance may be claimed. Those who move to unfurnished accommodation may be able to claim a special rehousing allowance towards the extra costs involved and in certain cases housing removal expenses will be met. Those selling a house and purchasing a new one near their job may qualify for up to three quarters of the house agent's and solicitor's fee within specified limits (for further details on mobility schemes, see NCSS, 1977 on which we have drawn for this section). The scheme came into effect on 1st April 1972, and during its first year 18,557 persons gained assistance. In the year ending 31st March 1976, 15,707 moves were supported by the scheme at a cost of a little under £6m, although this sum includes monies spent on the job search scheme, the key workers scheme, and the nucleus labour force scheme. (*Hansard*, 1977i, col. 676)

Conclusion

Early in 1977 the Secretary of State for Employment informed the House of Commons that the government job creation schemes had prevented a further 200,000 persons from joining the ranks of the unemployed. How did he arrive at this total? From the detailed analysis above of each of the job creation measures, it is clear that the Minister must have been referring to the success of the Temporary Employment Subsidy. We saw that by January 1977 nearly 185,000 workers had been covered by this scheme. Yet we do not know to what extent this scheme has been successful in preventing these workers from joining the numbers of unemployed as opposed to sparing them temporarily from this fate. Yet none of the other projects come anywhere near the success of the TES in achieving even this limited objective. For example whilst the Job Creation Programme has provided some 50,000 jobs since September 1975, only 10,000 or so unemployed people come within the programme at any one moment. It affords a short interlude of work in a much longer period of unemployment. We have also seen that the work experience programme has so far covered only 4,623 persons. Likewise the community industry scheme has helped eight and a half thousand young people while the job swap project seems fated to pay a tax free allowance to unemployed persons providing they withdraw their names from the unemployment register. One very important lesson therefore stands out from all the efforts the government has made in this field. Welcome as the job creation measures are, the evidence clearly demonstrates that these new initiatives only have a very limited effect on the overall level of employment and any effect they do have in preventing persons becoming unemployed may be only temporary. This moves our discussion on to ways in which we can once again bring about full employment, and this is the theme we tackle in the final chapter.

10 The return to full employment

Frank Field

Previous chapters in this book have exposed the major flaws in the arguments which support the running of the economy at a high level of unemployment. We have seen that the increase in numbers of unemployed cannot be accounted for, to any significant extent, by a rise in the numbers of voluntarily unemployed however one defines the word voluntary. Furthermore, the numbers of persons unemployed for structural reasons or who are 'between jobs' account for only one in three of those populating today's dole queues. Since 1974 we have seen a massive press-ganging of workers into Britain's conscript army of the unemployed to fight the war against inflation. Yet, as we show, there is no evidence to support the view that increasing the numbers of unemployed decreases the inflationary pressures in the British economy. Moreover, the price of this conscript army has now reached gigantic proportions. It is difficult to measure the cost of unemployment in human terms; in financial terms we have shown that the cost of running the British economy at a high level of unemployment since 1974 is already over £20 billion.

The need for counter-action is now paramount. In this chapter we look at the policies currently being pursued and evaluate their chance of success. We then look at an alternative strategy which has been put forward by those who argue for a return to the free market economy. As both the present strategy and the free-market approach offer little chance of returning to full employment, the second half of the chapter begins to outline a policy which would be most likely to achieve the triple goals outlined in the 1944 White Paper on full employment, namely, full employment combined with stable prices and a moderate annual increase in real living standards.

The government's goal

The government aims to reduce substantially the level of unemployment during the next couple of years. Speaking early in 1976 the Chancellor of the Exchequer commented that

If we are to reduce unemployment to 700,000 in 1979 — and certainly nothing less ambitious should be our objective — then our gross domestic product must grow at an average rate of $5^1/_2$ per cent over the preceding three years and manufacturing output must grow at about $8^1/_2$ per cent a year over the same period. (*Hansard*, 1976c, col. 255)

On 4 August 1976 the National Economic Development Council unanimously agreed a paper entitled 'Improved Industrial Performance Scenario' which provided for 'a sufficiently rapid return to full employment, based on the expansion of manufacturing industry through increased investment and higher productivity.' The projected growth rates for gross domestic product are detailed in Table 10.1.

TABLE 10.1 *Projected growth rates necessary to reduce unemployment to 700,000 by 1979*

% growth on previous year	1976	1977	1978	1979
GDP (factor cost)	3·75	5·5	5·5	3·75
Public consumption	3·75	0	0	0
Export of goods	11·25	14·25	13·25	10
Manufacturing output	4·5	11	10·5	6
Manufacturing investment	−5·75	21·25	27·5	11·5

To what extent are these targets being met? The crucial assumption behind the government's target of reducing unemployment to 700,000 by 1979 is an expansion of job opportunities in manufacturing industry through export-led growth. This assumption itself is based on predictions about the growth in world trade as well as the ability of British exporters to win an increasing share of the world market.

In July 1976 the Chancellor forecast that the economy would grow at an annual rate of 4·5 per cent over 18 months beginning from the first half of 1976. Manufacturing industry was expected to expand output at 8·5 per cent over the same period. Towards the end of 1976 the Treasury began to issue information suggesting that these forecasts were too optimistic. The October Treasury prediction was that growth during 1977 would be at about only half the earlier projection. Even so this forecast was far more optimistic than those of many independent research organisations.

In early 1977 the Treasury released their preliminary estimate of the increase in gross domestic product (GDP) during the previous year. The improved industrial performance scenario agreed at NEDC required an increase of GDP at 3·75 per cent during that year. The provisional estimate showed that during 1976 the GDP index rose by only 1 per cent.

Additional information suggests the target increase of exports during 1976 of 11·25 per cent is also unlikely to have been achieved. The reasons for this failure are clear. In August of that year the National Institute of Economic and Social Research (NIESR) reported that 'The recovery in UK output is clearly under way, against a background of a world recovery more rapid that we previously anticipated.' By November the NIESR review commented 'in fact output had stopped rising .... This pause in recovery has not been confined to Britain: it has happened in many industrial countries, including the United States, Germany and Japan.' (NIESR, 1976)

Unless there is an unexpected recovery in world trade, and this opportunity is seized by Britain's exporters, it will be impossible for the government to achieve a reduction in unemployment to the target level of 700,000 by 1979. Indeed, there are two additional factors now at work which make the target reduction in unemployment even more difficult to fulfil.

The first additional force which seems set to undermine the assumption underlying the government's calculations is that any increase in output is unlikely to come mainly from increased productivity rather than an expansion in the numbers of employed. Indeed the view of the Treasury now is that this should be so. In the Sir Ellis Hunter memorial lecture in November 1976, Mr Alan Lord, Second Permanent Secretary at the Treasury and responsible for the domestic economy sector, set out the case for making British exports more competitive by securing a real increase in productivity. Mr Lord was quite clear what effect this would have on the level of unemployment. 'In the short run, this means that for a given output we shall need a good deal less labour and new investment so there will be an increase in the underlying rate of unemployment.' (*The Times*, 11 November 1976)

Similar increases in productivity, with inconsequential effects on the level of unemployment, were outlined in papers prepared for the February meeting of the National Economic Development Council. An overall report which went to the NEDC meeting from thirty-three sector working parties states that their industries expect to be able to boost output by £36 billion over the next four years. The thirty-three sectors account for around 40 per cent of British manufacturing and employ one-eighth of all workers. This improved performance requires a 30 per cent increase in output over the rest of the decade. This forecast, however, is not based on market surveys but on the views of the employers and unionists on each of the working parties. Such an increase in output would easily set a postwar record in this country, but even so the working parties were clear that this trend would not provide many new jobs. 'The main thrust is expected to come from companies working at full capacity, and not much below it as at present, much higher productivity per worker, and the introduction of labour saving machinery.' (*Observer*, 30 January 1977)

The second force at work which is likely to increase unemployment between now and the end of the decade is the unexpected growth in the size of the labour force. If we compare the period from now up until 1981, and compare this with the trend from 1971 to 1976, the following changes stand out. It is expected that the total labour supply will increase from 1976 to 1981 by 774,000 persons to almost 26 million. This compares with an increase of 168,000 in the previous five years. Second, the number of men in the labour force, which fell between 1971 and 1976, is projected to increase by around 220,000. Third, the projections forecast an increase in the number of married women in the labour force of more than half a million. Fourth, the number of young people leaving school will increase between now and 1980, whereas their numbers were stable during the past five years.

Reporting on the effect of these changes, the Manpower Services Commission estimate that the total labour supply will reach about 25·8 million in 1980, a year after the government hopes to achieve a reduction of unemployment to 700,000.

> If both these figures are achieved, there must be jobs for 25·1 million people. It is estimated that at the beginning of 1976 about 24·2 million jobs were filled by the employed labour force, so the 'gap' between 1976 and 1980 totals about 900,000 jobs. (MSC, 1976,p.14)

These calculations show the need for 400,000 new jobs, to match the increase in the labour supply, together with an additional half a million new jobs, to reduce the unemployment level of 1·2 million in January 1976 to the target level of 700,000. However, since these calculations were undertaken, the numbers of unemployed have risen by 300,000. Therefore to reach a target level of unemployment of 700,000 by 1979 requires the creation of 1·2 million new jobs. We accept that the target level of 700,000 unemployed should be regarded as the objective of stage one in a policy to return to full employment. How can we best achieve this goal?

The difficulties of achieving a marked reduction in the numbers of unemployed by the end of the decade have now begun to permeate official statements (although these views have yet to be reflected in policy changes). As late as the end of September 1976 the Chancellor was able to assert: 'Unemployment will peak before the end of this year and will fall throughout next.' (*The Times*, 27 September 1976) However, by December the Prime Minister had begun to put over a very different message. At a meeting with Scottish trade union leaders in December 1976, Mr Callaghan informed his audience that the government would be introducing 'tough new economic measures that will increase unemployment during the next year.' (*The Times*, 9 December 1976) The tough economic measures accompanied the announcement of the government's successful negotiation of a new IMF loan to support sterling. Once these policy changes had been taken into account, the assessment by forecasting organisations showed a steep rise in the numbers of unemployed. By the end of December 1976 the stockbrokers Wood Mackenzie were forecasting a rise in unemployment to 1·7 million during 1977, while the Henley Centre for Forecasting predicted a further sharp increase, with adult unemployment rising to 2·5 million in 1982 on present policies. (*Financial Times*, 30 December 1976 and 14 February 1977)

On the assumption of a 1·5 per cent growth rate, a reported Treasury forecast has been a rise in the level of unemployment to 1,750,000. It is not surprising, therefore, that when the Secretary of State for Employment was asked 'would you totally rule out .... the figure of two million unemployed?' he answered: 'No, I am not going to totally pooh-pooh any figures. Nobody can be confident at this stage that we've solved, internally, the recession problem.' (*Daily Telegraph*, 5 February 1977) An even more gloomy prospect was put forward in a paper prepared for the Labour Party's Finance and Economic Affairs Committee. This Committee, which is served by outside experts such as Lord Balogh and Robert Nield, forecast 2·5 million unemployed by 1980. (*Observer*, 21 November 1976)

The free market approach

The need to consider an alternative strategy to the present one being pursued is therefore urgent. One such alternative has been put forward by the Confederation of British Industry with the aim of creating 'not less than a million new jobs'. (CBI, 1976 p.71) The CBI approach to a return to full employment is given in a manifesto centring on the advantages of a free market economy. We will therefore turn and examine the changes being called for by those who believe that 'the allocation of resources is most efficiently carried out when market forces are allowed to operate as freely as possible.' (*ibid.*, p.7)

In the first place the free marketeers maintain 'there is no economic justification for price controls.' (*ibid.*, p.20) The CBI maintains that price controls 'reduce investment, employment and discourage improvements in industrial efficiency ... their only justification has been as a politically necessary quid pro quo for wage restraint. But as they are harmful to the interests of all this has been a poor bargain on all sides.' (*ibid.*, p.20) Although the CBI does not call for the scrapping of price controls, this is implicit in a package of reforms.

Second, there is a call for increased profitability. *The Road to Recovery* notes that investment in manufacturing industry has to increase by no less than 70 per cent in real terms between 1976 and 1979 in order to fulfil one of the NEDC targets set out in scenario two. Investment will increase if prices are allowed to rise and the burden of taxation on companies reduced. The CBI set a target of a reduction in public expenditure by 1979/80 'of around £3 billion at 1975/6 prices'. But how this will have an immediate effect on company liquidity is unclear from their proposals. Much emphasis is put on explaining the case against a wealth tax which has yet to be introduced. Likewise there is a powerful plea for a reappraisal of the capital transfer tax (*ibid.*, pp.45-6), and the effect of the combination of the capital gains tax and capital transfer tax which amounts to 'a serious disincentive'. (*ibid.*, p.45) Surprisingly, the only positive proposals for changes in taxation which may have an immediate affect on companies is an increase in VAT, and the reduction of personal taxation. (*ibid.*, p.45)

The third ingredient in the policy of allowing market forces to operate freely is a substantial reduction in the burden of taxation on the managerial class. The CBI maintains that 'Unless there are substantial reductions in taxation of higher earned incomes our best managerial talent may consider that hard work and dedication are not worthwhile and that they would gain better recognition in countries with more favourable tax policies.' (*ibid.*, p.43). The main tax proposals are to bring down the top marginal rate on earned income to 60 per cent while at the same time guaranteeing full indexation of tax thresholds, personal allowances and starting levels of the higher rate bands.

The CBI's belief in the efficiency of a free market does not immediately extend to the settling of pay claims. It believes that incomes policy over the past couple of years has built up pressures which could result in a pay explosion. The CBI calculates that the restoration of differentials of all above the lowest paid to the levels of July 1975 will increase the pay bill by 6 to 7 per cent, and this does not allow for any further increase for the lowest paid. (*ibid.*, p.17) The cost of consolidating the earnings supplements allowed for during the last two years will add another 2 or 3 per cent to the national pay bill (*ibid.*, p.17). This leads the CBI to conclude 'a premature return to the old kind of free collective bargaining against the background of (these) pay pressures ... would be highly dangerous.' (*ibid.*, p.18) Furthermore, 'The Government should state clearly at an early stage that no return to free and unfettered collective bargaining is possible.' (*ibid.*, p.20) Meanwhile, the call is for discussions to reform the way pay increases are determined, and the CBI believes that such a clear statement of intent from the government against any return to 'unfettered collective bargaining', far from hindering discussions aimed at a more rational way of determining rewards, 'would give added impetus to them'. (*ibid.*, p.20)

The CBI maintains that the effect of implementing these proposals will mean a reduction in the rate of inflation, an increased resistance to imports and a corresponding effort in building up exports of both visible and invisible goods. Does past experience suggest that these goals will be achieved, and in particular how well will these export targets be met?

To achieve the NEDC scenario targets on employment in 1979 requires over 14 per cent growth in export volume in 1977 and over 13 per cent in 1978. This surge on the export front will require a reversal of past trends. For example, the UK share of the world trade declined from 8·5 per cent in 1955 to under 5 per cent twenty years later. Likewise, the cornerstone of the free market approach to achieving a million new jobs is an export-led boom. But the behaviour of exporters over the past few years casts serious doubts on whether this can be considered a serious possibility. The major devaluation of the currency which began to occur in the middle of 1975 has not led to a corresponding increase in the volume of exports. Sterling depreciated by about 20 per cent from the last quarter of 1975 to the end of September 1976. UK export prices went up about the same amount. The price of imports into the UK increased also by about 20 per cent.

> So the price of foreign manufactured goods entering the United
> Kingdom must have been *held roughly constant* in foreign countries'
> currency terms (although inflation was occurring abroad, as well as in
> the UK), and British exporters were marking up the sterling price of
> their exports roughly in line with the devaluation. (NALGO, 1977, p.9)

This trend has continued. Exports of goods rose by 8·5 per cent between 1975 and 1976 while their value increased by over 13 per cent. More importantly, sterling prices of exports rose by 21 per cent during the same period. Commenting on this information, the National Institute records 'These large increases seem to reflect a more active attitude towards pricing policies in export markets, which are becoming more profitable as sterling depreciation and domestic price restraint continue.' (NIESR, 1977, p.9) Put another way, exporters are preferring to maintain prices rather than reduce them as the exchange rate falls.

Both these pieces of information suggest that exporters prefer to take higher profits on a given level of exports, rather than expand their export base, thereby by giving rise to a possible increase in employment in this country. Even if the free marketeers' approach to regaining full employment could gain wide political acceptance, which is itself doubtful given some of the measures they are proposing, their approach is flawed once one looks at the evidence of how the market operates in practice. We, therefore, turn to propose an alternative way of guaranteeing a return to full employment. Success on this front will make a major difference to the happiness of millions of people who at present live in the shadow of unemployment. It is also in society's interest to pursue more vigorously a return to full employment. We have seen in Chapter 6 that the cost to the nation of growing unemployment since 1974 has been £20 billion. Full employment will regain some of the lost wealth which can be transferred into rebuilding our industrial base. How can we best break out of the present vicious circle of high unemployment, a commensurate drop in national income and the considerable loss of human dignity which worklessness entails in our country?

A policy for imports

Chapter 8, which analysed the causes of unemployment, showed that the major reason was an inadequate aggregate demand. We rejected, however, a 'simple' reflationary approach to regaining full employment, as the effect on the balance of payments would be catastrophic. The British economy has a lust for imports which is particularly pronounced as the economy moves back to full employment. This is a predeliction which is not so common in the economies of our competitors, and one way of making this comparison is to look at the demand for imports as national income rises. In doing so we find that for every 1 per cent increase in national income, imports rise in total by 1·8 per cent. This compares with 1·6 per cent in France and 1·3 per cent in Germany. (TUC, 1975a, p.48) The effect of this disproportionate propensity to import on our balance of payments as we move back to a full employment position has been detailed by the Cambridge Economic Policy Group. If we had expanded demand in order to return to a full employment level, which they define as 650,000 (a target level given purely for illustration), and if no counter-measures had been taken, the deficit on the balance of payments in 1975 would have been £4-£4·5 billion. Furthermore, as we can see from Table 10.2, imports are accounting for an increasing share of the GNP, even when the economy stagnates. This evidence suggests that greater attention should be given to the failure of British industry to hold its own, let alone improve its share in the home market.

In its *Economic Review* of 1975 the TUC divided UK imports into three main groups. The first consisted of those items which cannot be produced in the UK at all or in the quantity required for home consumption. These include food, beverages, tobacco, fuel and basic industrial material, which accounted for 47 per cent of the visible import bill in 1975. The second group of imports consists of semi-manufactured goods. The TUC notes that some of these items could not be replaced by UK products although within this second grouping, which accounts for 26 per cent of our visible import bill in 1975, are chemical products, textiles, yarns and fibres, motor-car components, electrical components,

TABLE 10.2 *Imports as a percentage of GDP at factor cost*

	Total imports (balance-of-payments basis) %	Total imports minus food, tobacco, fuels and basic materials (balance-of-payments basis)%
1970	18·2	9·8
1971	17·4	9·4
1972	17·9	10·3
1973	22·2	13·2
1974	28·7	15·5
1975	23·6	13·0
1976	26·0*	15·0*

*Provisional estimate

(*Source*: Hansard, 1977h, col. 592)

steel, paper and board. Some import substitution could occur here as many home industries have laid off considerable numbers of workers, while at the same time placing others on short time. The third category of imports, which accounted for 27 per cent of our visible import bill in 1975, is made up of finished manufactures. Within this category we find motor cars, motor cycles, clothing, footwear, cutlery, and domestic appliances for which UK subsitutes are, or could be, made available. It is within this third group of goods that we find increasing penetration of the home market by imports, and a corresponding failure on the export front. For example, in the second quarter of 1976, imports of motor vehicles and transport equipment rose by 12 per cent while exports fell by 2·5 per cent. (Ham, 1976, p.193) The increasing penetration of home markets by foreign manufactured goods has led to a significant loss of employment over the past few years. As we can see from Table 10.3 the number of jobs lost in the industries listed accounts for twice the number of jobs temporarily safeguarded or created by the whole of the government's job creation programme.

The major advantage of adopting an import control strategy is that it allows the government to deal separately with any balance-of-payments deficit while at the same time increasing aggregate demand. Imports can be held down to a level our export trade will finance, while home demand is expanded in line with the increasing supply of home-produced goods and services. In addition investment policy can be dovetailed to the demand for import substitution and this policy can be promoted by the National Enterprise Board if the private sector fails to deliver on this front. We need therefore to consider what ways are open to the government to limit imports without risking a major backlash from our trading partners?

In the first place the government should pursue a more active anti-dumping policy. Both employers and trade unionists complain of the considerable delay before action is taken against countries who are selling goods in Britain at a price below that charged in their own domestic market. Those who claim that goods are being dumped onto the British market have to satisfy three criteria. The first is that the imports are being sold at an artificially low price, second, that this is causing material injury to UK industry and third, that it is in the national interest to impose anti-dumping duties. As a first step to countering the considerable penetration of the home market by countries pursuing a dumping policy the Department of Trade, which is responsible for issuing any anti-dumping orders, should be much more willing to impose a three-month provisional duty where industry representatives put forward a *prima facie* case that dumping is occurring. Both the use of this provisional duty, and the longer term arrangements, are covered by GATT.

TABLE 10.3 *Employment decrease in selected manufacturing industries.*

	Nov. 1973 (000s)	Nov. 1975 (000s)	Jobs lost (000s)	%
Radio and electronic components	141·6	128·3	13·3	9·3
Broadcast receiving and sound reproducing equipment	70·9	52·0	18·9	26·6
Domestic electrical appliances	71·8	66·0	5·8	8·0
'Other' electrical goods	144·2	118·8	25·4	17·6
Motor vehicle manufacturing	507·5	441·2	66·3	13·0
Cutlery, spoons, forks and plated tableware	14·2	13·4	0·8	5·6
Bolts, nuts, screws, rivets etc.	39·3	34·7	4·6	11·7
Textiles of which:	544·4	494·9	49·5	9·0
cotton spinning	64·0	51·3	12·7	19·8
woollen and worsted	101·8	88·8	13·0	12·7
Hosiery and knitted goods	125·7	113·1	12·6	10·0
Clothing and footwear of which:	404·7	386·5	18·2	4·5
footwear	86·3	77·1	9·2	10·6
Paper and board	68·8	63·5	5·3	7·7
Packaging products	89·3	80·0	9·3	10·4
All manufacturing	7,678·7	7,293·2	385·5	5·0

(*Source*: TUC 1975a, p.52)

The second move should be for the government to impose temporary selective quotas where they can show that imports are leading to disruption of employment. As the TUC notes, temporary selective quotas are required to prevent any increase in the volume of motor cars, motor car components, electrical components, cutlery, textiles, clothing and footwear imports, as job losses in these industries have been considerable and import penetration, in some instances, has increased over the past couple of years. (TUC, 1975a, p.51) Again, as temporary selective quotas are covered by GATT, there should not be any retaliatory action by our trading partners.

Third, the government should impose the additional controls required to allow GNP to grow at 5·5 per cent in 1977 (or as near to this target as the value of our exports allows), the growth rate required to reduce unemployment to around 700,000 in the forseeable future. A 5·5 per cent growth rate without import controls would have a catastrophic effect on the balance of payments as imports would grow by over 20 per cent per annum. The government must therefore set import ceilings and, as it will be necessary to allow more imports of capital goods and semi-manufactures to an increasing extent in the early stages of a return to full employment, this policy will require that the volume of inessential imports should decline.

It is maintained by some critics that a policy of controlling the volume of imports in line with what we can pay for from our export earnings would invite retaliation. But it is difficult to see how our trading partners could implement any such threat. We have a substantial trading deficit with the three countries most likely to be affected by any controls. The largest single deficit is with West Germany, which had a trading surplus with us of £744 million in 1975 — a part of a £912 million deficit with EEC countries. The figure for Japan stood at £377 million and for the USA at £226 million. As one body has noted,

> these deficits mean that if the EEC, Japan or the USA attempt to
> retaliate against UK import control by cutting their imports from the
> UK they would have more to lose as their exports to us are more
> valuable than our exports to them. This clearly reduces the chances of
> retaliation. (*Labour Research*, 1976b, p.263)

In winning international approval for its policy, the government would also be able to quote the protective measures our trading partners have themselves taken in the recent past. For example, in August 1971 the USA devalued the dollar and imposed a 10 per cent special import tariff. None of the US trading partners imposed any reprisals whatsoever. In May 1974 the Italian government imposed an import deposit scheme. None of the EEC partners took any retaliatory action. Indeed, shortly afterwards the Italians negotiated an £800 million loan from the

Germans. In 1975 the French imposed unilaterally a 12 per cent tax on Italian wine; Italy confined herself to verbal protests. (For further details, see TUC, 1975b.)

Conclusion

Beveridge defined full employment as

> having always more vacant jobs than unemployed men, not slightly fewer jobs. It means that the jobs are to be at fair wages, of such a kind, and so located that the unemployed men can reasonably be expected to take them; it means by consequence, that the normal lag between losing one job and finding another will be very short. (1944, p.18)

Unemployment is now such a serious problem in Britain that this chapter has been concerned with outlining a policy which offers the hope of achieving a significant reduction in the number of unemployed by the end of the decade — a much more modest target than the one set by Beveridge. Implicit in this argument has been the need for a second round of initiatives to achieve the full-employment target set by Beveridge. It is a sign of both the extent of unemployment, and the structural problems in the British economy, that it is impossible to foresee, and unrealistic to advocate, a return to full employment by the end of the decade.

We have seen that, although the government aims to reduce unemployment to 700,000 by 1979, there is little chance of this being achieved. Already government spokesmen 'have repeatedly stressed that the figure of 700,000 was an ambitious target, not a forecast.' (*Hansard*, 1977a, col. 518) Yet we have suggested that far from achieving a reduction in unemployment a number of forces are at work which may result in an increase in unemployment towards the 2 million mark by the end of the decade.

One clear alternative to the present strategy has been put forward by those who believe in the working of the free market. However, as we have shown, while this alternative is unlikely to command wide public support, it also shares an additional disadvantage with the present strategy. It is unlikely to work. Its central assumption is of export-led growth at a time when all the evidence highlights the failure of our exporters to win an increasing share of the world market, despite the boost to our export price competitiveness following the very large fall in the value of sterling since the middle of 1975.

The only policy which holds out the chance of returning to full employment is one centring on import restrictions. This is not to say that import restrictions alone will bring about a marked change in this country's economic future. Three other major initiatives will need to be launched simultaneously. The first concerns investment policy. The overall aim is to increase employment by securing a greater share of the home market. Increased investment will need to be channelled first into import substituting industries. Over the last three years the whole community has suffered cuts in living standards (by agreeing to forgo some part of their wage or salary increases under incomes policy, and a pricing policy which allows half the cost of investment to be offset by raising prices) in order to raise company profitability and thereby investment. If the private sector fails to deliver with 'our investment' the case will effectively be made for direct intervention by the NEB.

In many industries, an increase in investment does not lead to a proportionate increase in the numbers of new jobs available. New capital is usually more productive than that which it replaces. If increased investment is going to increase employment it is important that the level of demand is also increasing, otherwise fewer workers will be employed to produce the same output. In the short run we also need to consider the question of job sharing. In Table 10.4 we present information gathered by Jeff Rooker on the amount of overtime work in selected industries, together with the numbers of registered unemployed. As we can see, a dramatic fall in unemployment would occur if working people worked only 40 hours a week. An even greater improvement would take place if the TUC resolution against workers holding two jobs was fully implemented, or the working week reduced or the length of holidays extended.

There is a simple reason however, why so little progress has been made on the worksharing front. Many, although not all, employees work excessive overtime in order to bring their wage packets up to a reasonable level. Excessive overtime is the siamese twin of low pay. If we update the TUC 1974 minimum wage target of £30 a week we arrive at a figure of around £45 a week. In 1976 over 3·8 million were earning less than this figure. If we are going to stand any chance of success in significantly reducing the amount of overtime worked, and thereby increase the numbers of jobs available, the government will have to initiate a much more determined campaign on low pay than we have hitherto seen. We have outlined elsewhere the main measures which this campaign will require. (See the concluding essay in Field, 1977.)

The third accompanying economic reform centres on incomes policy. Commenting on politicians, Jimmy Maxton is reported as saying that unless one is able to ride two horses at once, one shouldn't be part of a bloody circus. Some politicians and trade unionists appear to believe that it increases their political prowess to argue on the one hand for controlling the volume of imports, while on the other calling for free collective bargaining. We believe that working out a policy returning to full employment is a much more serious business than running a circus.

TABLE 10.4 *Extent of overtime – expressed in weeks – for each manufacturing sector together with the numbers of registered unemployed*

	Hours of overtime worked by operatives divided by 40: Week ended 14th August 1976	Unemployed on 12th August 1976
Food, drink and tobacco	48,200	38,962
Coal and petroleum products	2,100	2,270
Chemicals and allied industries	18,000	16,063
Metal manufacture	28,300	26,079
Mechanical engineering	46,400	39,752
Instrument engineering	3,900	4,661
Electrical engineering	19,500	30,496
Shipbuilding and marine engineering	13,400	8,332
Vehicles	29,000	27,079
Metal goods not elsewhere specified	25,500	36,651
Textiles	16,800	27,923
Leather, leather goods and fur	1,400	3,552
Clothing and footwear	2,200	20,994
Bricks, pottery, glass, cement, etc.	18,200	14,417
Timber, furniture, etc.	11,400	16,557
Paper, printing and publishing	24,900	18,570
Other manufacturing industries	14,300	17,859

(*Source*: *Hansard*, 1977j, cols 237–8)

Discussing rationally how much the country can afford each year in increasing the rewards of its work people, and those who are unable to work and are dependant on benefit, will be an important part of any new economic strategy. As Barbara Wootton has commented, it is difficult to understand the logic 'which does not allow a citizen to build a garage in his own backyard without official permission, and yet is content to leave the crucial matter of pay settlements to a system in which the weak go to the wall and also have to pay the price of the success of the strong'. (Wootton, 1974b, p.18)

We argued in Chapter 7 that there was no evidence to support the view that inflation in this country has been wage induced. However, it would be wrong to deduce from this that excessive wage claims could not become an engine force behind inflation. The debate about what constitutes a fair reward for the job, and how these rewards relate to the work carried out by other members of society, is going to be one of the central questions of political economy we will face as a community in the remainder of this century and, no doubt, well beyond.

By explaining the need for an incomes policy we are not trying to invent a euphemism for annihilating one of the central activities of trade unions — although we accept that this is why a number of groups support an incomes policy. If we are to achieve a permanent incomes policy it will be along the lines proposed by Barbara Wootton. (See Wootton, 1974a) This approach allows for a planned growth in income to be linked with trade unions arguing at a national level not only about what share of the increase in national income should be allocated to wages and salaries and, we would argue, the social wage, but how this should be further distributed between the major bargaining groups. This approach would allow unions within industries to be free to argue for a distribution of the increase which best suits the particular needs of that industry.

Quoted at the beginning of this volume is the comment that no man can live with himself for long if he knows he is unwanted. Such is the fate of the unemployed. This book has attempted to show the size of the real unemployment problem, the poverty and misery which is still associated with it, the cost to the community, as well as considering how best we as a community can return to full employment. There are now overwhelmingly powerful economic, political, but above all human arguments for adopting the new policy for full employment which this chapter has described.

Bibliography

Beveridge, Lord (1944), *Full Employment in a Free Society*, London, Allen & Unwin.

Blackaby, F. (1976), 'The target rate of unemployment', in G.D.N. Worswick (ed.), *The Concept and Measurement of Involuntary Unemployment*, London, Allen & Unwin.

Boulet, J. and Bell, A. (1973), *Unemployment and Inflation*, London, Economic Research Council.

Bosanquet, N. and Doeringer, P.B. (1973), 'Is there a dual labour market in Great Britain?' *Economic Journal*, June.

Bowers, J.K. and Harkness, D. (1974), 'Duration of unemployment by age', *School of Economics Discussion Paper Series*, 8, University of Leeds.

Bowers, J.K. and Harkness, D. (1976), 'A time series of duration of unemployment by age and sex', *School of Economics Discussion Paper 27*, University of Leeds.

British Labour Statistics, Historical Abstracts, 1886–1968 (1971), London, HMSO.

British Labour Statistics Year Book 1971 (1973), London, HMSO.

British Labour Statistics Year Book 1974 (1976), London, HMSO.

Brittan, S. (1975), *Second Thoughts on Full Employment*, London, Centre for Policy Studies.

Brittan, S. (1976), 'Full employment policy: a reappraisal' in G.D.N. Worswick (ed.), *The Concept and Measurement of Involuntary Unemployment*, London, Allen & Unwin.

Burton, J. (1972), *Wage Inflation*, London, Macmillan.

Centre for Policy Studies (1976), press release, 'What the July unemployment figures really show', 25 July.

Cheshire, P.C. (1973), *Regional Unemployment Differences in Great Britain*, Cambridge, CUP.

Community Relations Commission (1974), *Unemployment and Homelessness*, London, HMSO.

Confederation of British Industry (1976), *The Road to Recovery*.

Cripps, T.F. and Tarling, R.J. (1974), 'An analysis of the duration of male unemployment 1932–1973', *Economic Journal*, June.

Daniel, W.W. (1972), 'Whatever Happened to the Workers in Woolwich?' London, PEP.

Daniel, W.W. (1974), *A National Survey of the Unemployed*, London, PEP.

Daniel, W.W. and Stilgoe, E. (1976), 'Towards an American way of unemployment', *New Society,* 12 February.

Dean, A.J.H. (1976), 'Unemployment among school leavers: an analysis of the problem', *National Institute Economic Review*, November.

DE (1973a), 'Duration of unemployment', *Gazette*, February.

DE (1973b), 'Trends in the composition of the unemployed', *Gazette*, March.

DE (1974a), 'Characteristics of the unemployed: sample survey June 1973', *Gazette*, March.

DE (1974b), 'Characteristics of the unemployed: analysis by occupation', *Gazette*, May.

DE (1974c), 'Statistics of unemployment in the United Kingdom, *Gazette*, June.

DE (1975a), *Gazette*, September.

DE (1975b), *Gazette*, November.

DE (1976a), *Gazette*, March.

DE (1976b), 'Temporary employment subsidy', *Gazette*, May.

DE (1976c), 'Duration of unemployment and age of unemployed', *Gazette*, August.

DE (1976d), *Gazette,* September.

DE (1976e), *Gazette*, November.

DE (1976f), 'The unregistered unemployed in Great Britain', *Gazette*, December.

DE (1976g), 'Disabled people', *Gazette*, December.

DE (1977), *Gazette*, February.

DHSS (1975), *Social security statistics*, London, HMSO.

Doeringer, P.B. and Piore, M.J. (1971), *Internal Labour Markets and Manpower Analysis*, Lexington, Mass, Lexington Books.

Donnison, D. (1976), 'The poverty trap', Lecture delivered at North London Polytechnic, 7 December.

Economic Trends, Annual Supplement, 1976.

Economic Trends, February 1977.

Field, F. (1971), 'Clydeside: the cost of putting men out of work', *Tribune*, 2 July.

Field F. (ed.) (1977), *Are Low Wages Inevitable?* Nottingham, Russell Press.

Fisher, Sir H. (1973), *Report of the Committee on Abuse of Social Security Benefits*, London, HMSO.

Flemming, J. (1976), *Catch 76?* London, IEA.

Friedman, M. (1968), 'The role of monetary policy', *American Economic Review*, March.

Friedman, M. (1975), *Unemployment Versus Inflation?* London, IEA.

General Household Survey 1973 (1976), London, HMSO.

Giddens, A. (1973), *The Class Structure of the Advanced Societies*, London, Hutchinson.

Gordon, D.M. (1972), *Theories of Poverty and Underemployment: Orthodox, Radical and Dual Labour Market Perspectives*, Lexington, Mass., Lexington Books.

Gujarati, D. (1972), 'The behaviour of unemployment and unfilled vacancies: Great Britain, 1958–1971, *Economic Journal*, March.

Ham, A. (1976), 'An alternative economic strategy, *Labour Research*, September.

Hansard (1975a), 28 October, vol. 898.

Hansard (1975b) 10 December, vol. 902.

Hansard (1976a), 4 February, vol. 904.

Hansard (1976b), 12 February, vol. 905.

Hansard (1976c), 9 March, vol. 907.

Hansard (1976d), 17 March, vol. 907.

Hansard (1976e), 24 May, vol. 912.

Hansard (1976f), 21 June, vol. 913.

Hansard (1976g), 2 August, vol. 916.

Hansard (1976h), 6 August, vol. 916.

Hansard (1976i), 15 October, vol. 917.

Hansard (1976j), 27 October, vol. 918.

Hansard (1976k), 28 October, vol. 918.

Hansard (1976l), 1 November, vol. 918.

Hansard (1976m), 18 November, vol. 919.

Hansard (1976n), 6 December, vol. 922.

Hansard (1976p), 23 December, vol. 923.

Hansard (1977a), 12 January, vol. 923.

Hansard (1977b), 21 January, vol. 924.

Hansard (1977c), 24 January, vol. 924.

Hansard (1977d), 7 February, vol. 925.

Hansard (1977e), 11 February, vol. 925.

Hansard (1977f), 14 February, vol. 926.

Hansard (1977g), 18 February, vol. 926.

Hansard (1977h), 23 February, vol. 926.

Hansard (1977i), 24 February, vol. 926.

Hansard (1977j), 2 March, vol. 927.

Hansard (1977k), 3 March, vol. 927.

Hansard (1977l), 19 April, vol. 930.

Healey, D. (1975), Treasury press release, 16 October.

Henry, S.G.B., Sawyer, M.C. and Smith, P. (1976), 'Model of inflation in the UK', *National Institute Economic Review*, August.

Hill, M.G., Harrison, R.M., Sargent, A.V. and Talbot, V. (1973), *Men Out of Work*, Cambridge, CUP.

Hines, A.G. (1964), 'Wage inflation in the United Kingdom, 1893–1961', *Review of Economic Studies*, vol. 31.

Hines, A.G. (1976), 'The micro-economic foundations of wages and employment theory' in G.D.N. Worswick (ed.), *The Concept and*

Measurement of Involuntary Unemployment, London, Allen & Unwin.

Holt, C.C. (1969), 'Improving the labour market trade off between inflation and unemployment', *American Economic Review*, vol. LIX.

Hughes, J.J. (1975), 'How should we measure unemployment? *British Journal of Industrial Relations*, vol. XIII, no. 3.

Hughes, J. (1976), 'Incomes policy: the case for a third phase', *The Banker*, December.

Joseph, Sir Keith (1974), 'Getting to grips with the catastrophic effects of inflation', *The Times*, 6 September.

Keynes, J.M. (1936), *The General Theory of Employment, Interest and Money*, London, Macmillan.

Labour Research (1976a), 'Unemployment', October.

Labour Research (1976b), 'Loss of balance', December.

Liebow, E. (1970), 'No man can live with the terrible knowledge that he is not needed', *New York Times Magazine*, 5 April.

Pond, C., Field, F. and Winyard, S. (1976), *Trade Unions and Taxation*, London, WEA.

Mackay, D.I. and Reid, G.L. (1972), 'Redundancy, unemployment and manpower policies', *Economic Journal*, December.

Marsden, D. and Duff, E. (1975), *Workless*, Harmondsworth, Penguin.

Marshall, R. (1972), *Families Receiving Supplementary Benefit*, London, HMSO.

Meacher, M. (1974), *Scrounging on the Welfare*, London, Arrow.

Metcalfe, D. and Richardson, R. (1972), 'The nature and measurement of unemployment in the UK', *Three Banks Review*, March.

Manpower Services Commission (1976), *Towards a Comprehensive Manpower Policy*.

Ministry of Labour (1962), 'Characteristics of the unemployed' *Gazette*, April.

Ministry of Labour (1966), *Gazette*, April.

Mukherjee, S. (1974), *There's Work to be Done: Unemployment and Manpower Policies*, Manpower Services Commission, London, HMSO.

Mukherjee, S. (1976), *Unemployment Costs*, London, PEP.

NALGO (1976), *The Economic Situation and the Cuts in Public Expenditure*, London.

NAB (1951), *Report of the National Assistance Board*, London, HMSO.

NAB (1954), *Report of the National Assistance Board*, London, HMSO.

NAB (1956), *Report of the National Assistance Board*, London, HMSO.

National Council for Social Service (1977), *Briefing*, February.

NIESR (1976), *National Institute Economic Review*, November.

NIESR (1977), *National Institute Economic Review*, February.

Office of Population, Censuses and Surveys (1971), *Effects of the Redundancy Payments Act*, London, HMSO.

Office of Population, Censuses and Surveys (1974), *Population Projections 1973–2013*, London HMSO.

Paish, F.W. (1966), 'The limits of incomes policy' in F.W. Paish and J. Hennessy, *Policy for Incomes*, London, IEA.

Phillips, A.W. (1958), 'The relation between unemployment and the rate of change in money wages', *Economica, New Series*, vol. 25, November.

Pigou, A.C. (1933), *Theory of unemployment*, London, Cass.

Pratten, G.H. (1972), 'How higher wages can cause unemployment', *Lloyds Bank Review*, January.

Sinfield, A. (1970), 'Poor and out of work in Shields' in P. Townsend (ed.), *The Concept of Poverty*, London, Heinemann.

Sinfield, A. (1974), *Low take up of supplementary allowances by the unemployed*, mimeograph.

Sinfield, A. (1976), 'Social costs and the analysis of unemployment', in G.D.N. Worswick (ed.), *The Concept and Measurement of Involuntary Unemployment,* London, Allen & Unwin.

Smith, D.J. (1976), *Some Facts of Racial Disadvantage*, London, PEP.

Taylor, J. (1972), 'The behaviour of unemployment and unfilled vacancies: Great Britain, 1958–71, an alternative view', *Economic Journal*, December.

Treasury, 1976a, *Economic Progress Report*, October.

Treasury (1976b) 'Unemployment: the underlying picture', *Economic Progress Report*, 81, December.

Trevithick, J.A. (1976), 'Inflation, the natural unemployment rate and the theory of economic policy, *Scottish Journal of Political Economy*, February.

TUC (1975a), *Economic Review*.

TUC (1975b), 'Imports' – TUC memorandum to the Prime Minister, October 29.

Unemployment Assistance Board (1938), *Report of the Unemployment Assistance Board*, Cmd 6021, London, HMSO.

Unemployment Statistics (1972), Cmnd 5157, London, HMSO.

Unemployment Statistics (1972a), Final Report of the DE working party on the changed relationship between unemployment and vacancies, DE mimeograph.

Wedderburn, D. (1965), *Redundancy and the Railwaymen*, Cambridge, CUP.

Wedderburn, D. (1971), 'Unemployment in the seventies, *Listener*, 12 August.

Wilkinson, F. and Turner, H. (1975), 'The wage-tax spiral and labour militancy' in Jackson *et al. Do Trade Unions Cause Inflation?* CUP.

Wood, J.B. (1972), *How Much Unemployment?* London, IEA.

Worswick, G.D.N. (ed.), (1976), *The Concept and Measurement of Involuntary Unemployment*, London, Allen & Unwin.

Wootton, B. (1974a), *Incomes Policy, an Inquest and a Proposal*, London, Davis-Poynter.

Wootton, B. (1974b), Fair pay, relativities and a policy for incomes. The Twentieth Fawley Foundation Lecture, University of Southampton.

Index